Sporting with the Classics
The Latin Poetry of William Dillingham

Sporting with the Classics
The Latin Poetry of William Dillingham

ESTELLE HAAN

American Philosophical Society
Philadelphia • 2010

Transactions of the
American Philosophical Society
Held at Philadelphia
For Promoting Useful Knowledge
Volume 100, Part 1

Copyright ©2010 by the American Philosophical Society for its Transactions series.
All rights reserved.

Library of Congress Cataloging-in-Publication Data

Haan, Estelle.
  Sporting with the classics : the Latin poetry of William Dillingham / Estelle Haan.
    p. cm. — (Transactions of the American Philosophical Society held at Philadelphia for promoting useful knowledge ; v. 100, pt. 1)
  Includes bibliographical references and index.
  ISBN 978-1-60618-001-3
  1. Dillingham, William, 1617?-1689—Criticism and interpretation. 2. Latin poetry, Medieval and modern—England—History and criticism. I. Dillingham, William, 1617?-1689. Poems. English & Latin. Selections. II. Title.
  PA8485.D66Z66 2010
  791.43092'2—dc22
                         2010017091

ABOUT THE AUTHOR

Estelle Haan is Professor of English and Neo-Latin Studies at The Queen's University of Belfast. Her research interests lie mainly in links between English and neo-Latin poetry of the seventeenth and eighteenth centuries (in particular the Latin poetry of English poets). She is the author of *From Academia to Amicitia: Milton's Latin Writings and the Italian Academies* (American Philosophical Society, 1998); *Thomas Gray's Latin Poetry: Some Classical, Neo-Latin and Vernacular Contexts* (Collection Latomus, Brussels, 2000); *Andrew Marvell's Latin Poetry: From Text to Context* (Collection Latomus, Brussels, 2003); *Vergilius Redivivus: Studies in Joseph Addison's Latin Poetry* (American Philosophical Society, 2005); and *Classical Romantic: Identity in the Latin Poetry of Vincent Bourne* (American Philosophical Society, 2007). She is currently completing an edition of Milton's Latin and Greek poetry for Oxford University Press.

CONTENTS

About the Author
Preface
Acknowledgments
Introduction   1

Chapter 1:   Sporting with the Classics: *Suleianum*   17

Chapter 2:   Ringing Classical Bells: *Campanae Undellenses*   39

Chapter 3:   Two Classical Fables? From *Avicula* to Nemesis   49

Chapter 4:   A Horticultural Metamorphosis: *Sepes Hortensis*   61

Appendix 1   Willian Dillingham's Latin Poetry: 75
Latin Text and Facing English Translation

Appendix 2   "Suley Bowling Greene":
Bodl. MS Eng. Misc. d.1, ff 45-47   93

Appendix 3   Dillingham's Occasional Latin Verse   97

Bibliography   113
Index Nominum   119

PREFACE

This study focuses on the original Latin poetry of William Dillingham, a seventeenth-century editor, anthologist, and Vice-Chancellor of Cambridge University. It does so in an attempt to disprove claims that Dillingham's talent lay in criticism rather than in original composition, and that his Latin verse shows his complete independence of the old school of classical imitation. It has the twofold aim of highlighting both the classical and the contemporary intertexts with which this hitherto neglected poetry engages. It argues that far from constituting the leisurely product of a gentleman in rustic retirement, this is highly talented verse that "sports" with the classics in several ways: first in its self-consciously playful interaction with the Latin poets of Augustan Rome, chiefly Virgil and Ovid; second in its appropriation of a classical world and its linguistic medium to describe such seventeenth-century sports or pastimes as bowling, horticulture, and bell-ringing. It also foregrounds the pseudoromanticism surprisingly inherent in the work of a late-seventeenth-century poet, who, it is argued, discovered in his twilight years a neo-Latin inspirational Muse.

ACKNOWLEDGMENTS

I wish to thank the Queen's University Research and Scholarships Committee for funding trips to the British Library, London, and the Bodleian Library, Oxford, and the authorities of those institutions for permitting me to consult manuscripts and early printed books relevant to my research. I am indebted also to the Queen's University Library, especially its Special Collections and Inter-Library Loans divisions. A much abridged version of chapter 2 appeared in *Notes and Queries* (December 2007). It is expanded and reproduced here with permission.

Finally I wish to thank my husband, Tony Sheehan, Humanities Computing Manager at Queen's, for his technical assistance and advice throughout and also, and especially, for his support in so many ways. To him I dedicate this monograph as a small token of a very great love.

EH

INTRODUCTION

In 1678 there appeared in London a very new kind of anthology of neo-Latin verse. Unconnected to any single event, occasion, or political circumstance, and unaffiliated with any one university,[1] this collection confidently presented and indeed showcased neo-Latin poetry for its own sake. As such it can be seen both to mirror and take its place alongside the *Delitiae* collections (for Italy, France, Belgium, and Germany) that had appeared at the beginning of the century.[2] Bearing the rather elaborate title *Poemata Varii Argumenti Partim e Georgio Herberto Latine (Utcunque) Reddita, Partim Conscripta a Wilh. Dillingham, S.T.D.*, the volume is in fact a bipartite anthology, which is much more comprehensive than even this verbose title would suggest. Compiled by a certain William Dillingham,[3] Part One consists of Dillingham's Latin verse renderings of extracts from George Herbert's English poetry (*The Temple*),[4] and from Erasmus's Latin prose treatise *De Civilitate Morum Puerilium*,[5] as well as five original Latin poems by Dillingham on such

---

[1] Contrast the official poetry anthologies issued by Oxford and Cambridge to commemorate occasions of national significance or to lament the deaths of individuals. Examples of the latter are the three Cambridge and Oxford anthologies published on the death of Sir Philip Sidney in 1586/87.

[2] See, for example: *Delitiae Carminum Italorum Poetarum Huius Superiorisque Aevi* (Frankfurt, 1608); *Delitiae Carminum Poetarum Gallorum Huius Superiorisque Aevi* (Frankfurt, 1609); *Delitiae Carminum Poetarum Belgicorum Huius Superiorisque Aevi* (Frankfurt, 1612); *Delitiae Carminum Poetarum Germanorum Huius Superiorisque Aevi* (Frankfurt, 1612).

[3] On Dillingham, see W.H. Kelliher, *Oxford Dictionary of National Biography*, eds. H.C.G. Matthew and Brian Harrison (Oxford, 2004), sv William Dillingham, and 3-6 below.

[4] Dillingham renders Herbert's "The Church-Porch," "The Sacrifice," "Providence," "Charms and Knots," and "Mans Medley" into Latin verse in the poems *Perirrhanterium, Sacrificium, Providentia, Gryphi*, and *Gaudium*, at *Poemata Varii Argumenti Partim e Georgio Herberto Latine (Utcunque) Reddita, Partim Conscripta a Wilh. Dillingham, S.T.D.* (London, 1678), 1-23, 24-35, 35-42, 43 and 44 respectively. All quotations from Dillingham's Latin poetry are from this edition.

[5] See *De Civilitate Morum Puerilium Per D. Erasmum Roterodamum Libellus* (London, 1578) rendered by Dillingham into Latin hexameters entitled *De Moribus Puerorum* at *Poemata Varii Argumenti*, 45-56.

topics as the game of bowls,[6] the tolling of church bells,[7] the first flight of a fledgling bird,[8] a garden topiary,[9] and a hangman's stone with its associated folklore.[10] Part Two, however, moves far beyond the confines of England and its poets to embrace a broader spectrum of both classical and contemporary (or near contemporary) verse. Thus Virgil, Manilius, and Lucan sit quite happily alongside Theodore Beza, Marco Girolamo Vida, George Buchanan, Hugo Grotius, Desiderius Erasmus, Phineas Fletcher, and Thomas More.

The collection is pioneering in a number of respects: chiefly perhaps in its placing of neo-Latin poetry on an equal footing with that of the classics of ancient Rome, its recognition of neo-Latin verse as a distinct category of writing,[11] and its innovative situating of Anglo-Latin poetry within a wider continental context. Indeed the breadth of Part Two is quite stunning for its day and works on both a geographical and generic level. What is immediately apparent is that the language of classical Rome has become the poetic medium for a range of international "modern" neo-Latin writers (from Scotland, England, the Low Countries, and Italy) now for the first time collectively available in print. And the nationality of such authors is rather self-consciously highlighted. For example, Andrew Melvin and Thomas Rhaedus are both termed *Scoti*, whereas other writers are designated by their associated city: Phineas Fletcher *Cantabrigiensis*, Vida *Cremonensis*, Erasmus *Roterodamus*, and so on. The content is equally wide-ranging, embracing inter alia biblical material (reproduced in Latin metaphrase and paraphrase),[12] surprisingly

---

[6] *Suleianum* (*Poemata Varii Argumenti*, 56-59).

[7] *Campanae Undellenses* (*Poemata Varii Argumenti*, 60-64).

[8] *Avicula* (*Poemata Varii Argumenti*, 65-66).

[9] *Sepes Hortensis* (*Poemata Varii Argumenti*, 67).

[10] *Nemesis a Tergo* (*Poemata Varii Argumenti*, 68).

[11] Dillingham would be succeeded in this respect by Walter Savage Landor whose essay *Quaestio quamobrem Poetae Latini Recentiores Minus Legantur* likewise identifies neo-Latin verse as a distinct literary category and affords it due recognition as an international enterprise. See Walter Savage Landor, *Poemata et Inscriptiones* (London, 1847), 264-348.

[12] Cf. *Carmen Mosis, Deut. 32 per A. Melvinum* (*Poemata Varii Argumenti*, 69-77); *Jobi Capita Prima Tria et Postrema Quinque e Metaphrasti Poetica J.A. Thuani* (*Poemata Varii Argumenti*, 78-95); *Senectutis Effigies ex Eiusdem Metaphr. Poetica Capitis XII. Ecclesiastis* (*Poemata Varii Argumenti*, 96-97); *Theod. Bezae Praefatio Poetica in Psal. Davidis LL* (*Poemata Varii Argumenti*, 98-107); *Tho. Rhaedi*

juxtaposed with Latin poems on such topics as the game of chess,[13] the art of printing,[14] and the gunpowder plot.[15] As such it reveals an anthologist with a vision, a writer who saw himself and his fellow neo-Latin poets as taking their justified place in a tradition that not only looked back to the classical world, but also and essentially reinvented and appropriated that world and its language to suit contemporary subjects. But what of that anthologist, whose name is all too unfamiliar even to neo-Latinists in the twenty-first century? What of the pioneering vision that seems to have inspired this collection? As noted below, this vision was perhaps both the product and culmination of a seventeenth-century humanist, a versatile scholar, who was at various times editor, translator, preacher, biographer, anthologist, and, especially significant for the purposes of the present study, neo-Latin poet in his own right.

Born c. 1617 William Dillingham was the eldest son of Thomas Dillingham, rector of Barnwell All Saints, Northamptonshire. He received his preuniversity education at Barnwell Grammar School, from which he went up at the age of nineteen to Emmanuel College, Cambridge. There his roommate was William Sancroft (the future Archbishop of Canterbury), who would in fact succeed him as Master of Emmanuel and prove a lifelong friend, correspondent, and critic of his Latin poetry.[16] Having gained his BA in 1639, Dillingham was elected (in 1642) Fellow of Emmanuel. Indeed his close affiliation with university life is frequently attested by his correspondence with Sancroft. Writing (in Latin) to Sancroft in June 1642, he describes with empathetic

---

Paraphrasis Psalmi CIIII (*Poemata Varii Argumenti*, 107-109); *Historia Jonae, Carmine Paraphr. per Hug. Grotium* (*Poemata Varii Argumenti*, 109-118); *Eiusdem Paraphrasis in Tres Versus Postremos Cap X Proph. Jeremiae* (*Poemata Varii Argumenti*, 118-120).

[13] *M. Hieron. Vidae Cremonensis Scacchia Ludus* (*Poemata Varii Argumenti*, 134-154).

[14] *Tho. Rhaedi De Arte Typographica Carmen* (*Poemata Varii Argumenti*, 157-159).

[15] Phineas Fletcher, *Locustae* (*Poemata Varii Argumenti*, 208-234).

[16] It is interesting to note that Dillingham played a rather similar advisory role vis-à-vis Justinian Isham's verse-compositions. In a letter to Justinian he announces that he is returning "your excellent and elegant poem with some alterations; wherein if I have exceeded my commission, I must begg your pardon." He proceeds to state that he has only "mingled a little water with your inke, which if it make it thinner, it does also make it somewhat smoother." Cf. *The Diary of Thomas Isham of Lamport (1658-81), Kept by Him in Latin from 1671-1673 at His Father's Command*, trans. Norman Marlow, with notes and commentary by Sir Giles Isham (Farnborough, 1971), 82.

fondness the feverish excitement of the students preparing to leave as the end of term approaches, comparing them to birds about to take to flight.[17] He graduated MA in 1643, BD in 1650, and DD in 1655. In 1646 his English verses in praise of John Hall's Poems were included among the encomia prefixed to the Cambridge edition of Hall's poetry. Having been entrusted with the papers of Nathaniel Culverwell,[18] he published (in 1651) his *Spiritual Opticks* and (in 1652) an edition of his *The Light of Nature*, dedicating the latter to the Masters and Fellows of Emmanuel College.[19] He also edited from manuscript Theodore Bathurst's Latin verse-rendering of Spenser's *The Shepheardes Calender* (1653). But Dillingham frequently looked beyond the confines of England and her poets. For example, in 1647 we find him corresponding with the Dutch neo-Latin poet Daniel Heinsius, sending him gift-copies of his own works.[20] In 1653 he obtained the Mastership of Emmanuel College,[21] a position which he would hold until 1662. Despite evidence that the college did not fare particularly well during his mastership,[22] and that the students may in fact have been rather out of hand,[23] his Cambridge years

---

[17] Bodl. Tanner MS 63, f. 42: *Terminus Academiae usque ad diem praesentis Junii 13 prorogatur, processurus denuo protinus si res nostras in tuto positas intellexerimus; sed interim levant ales suas iuvenes ac si avolaturi ...*

[18] Cf. Dillingham, ed., Nathaniel Culverwell, *The Light of Nature* (London, 1652), Epistle Dedicatory A2ᵛ: "Having therefore the disposal of his papers committed to me by his nearest and dearest friends, and finding them to be of such worth and excellence as ought not to be smothered in obscurity ..."

[19] Kelliher, *ODNB* ad loc, notes that between 1656 and 1662 Dillingham's name "appeared as a syndic of the university press on licences for sixteen works."

[20] In a Latin letter dated 20 May 1647 Daniel Heinsius thanks Dillingham for such a gift: *Deauratum munus tuum, cum epistola illa quidem amicissima, sic ante tempus aliquod accepi.* (BL Sloane 1710, f.181).

[21] John Hacket sent Dillingham a congratulatory letter (6 April 1654). Cf. BL Sloane 1710, f. 197: *maxime cumulasti beneficio (Vir praestantissime) adeoque laetificabili nuntio perfudisti, quod ab humanissimis tuismet literis hausi Collegii vestri praefecturam tibi obtigisse.*

[22] E.S. Shuckburgh, *Emmanuel College* (London, 1904), 101, remarks: "... under his charge the College showed no sign of recuperation. The number of entries averaged only about twenty-five, and a College order regarding the stipend of the Head Lecturer and the fees to be paid by residents mentions that the proportion of sizars to pensioners was increasing."

[23] Shuckburgh, *Emmanuel College*, 102, states: "he was said to be more interested in his private studies and literary employments than in the government of the College.

are marked by a flurry of editorial activity. He published in 1657 the military Commentaries of Sir Francis Vere and an edition of the *Lexicon Geographicum* of Philip Ferrarius. In the late 1650s he married Elizabeth by whom he had three sons and a daughter. He was appointed Vice-Chancellor of the University in 1659, but his refusal to conform to the Act of Uniformity (1662) resulted in his automatic forfeiture (in August of that year) of all his Cambridge posts.[24] Shuckburgh remarks that "it was much to the credit of his honesty that he quitted [Cambridge] on conscientious grounds."[25] Nonetheless he continued to remain on good terms with his successor, William Sancroft, to whom he addressed a very generous letter.[26] As Shuckburgh notes, "It would not be easy for a dispossessed man to write to his successor with more magnanimous kindness or with better temper."[27] Likewise his interest in and

---

Certainly the entrances were low during his mastership, and the number of 'admonitions' is rather above the average, as though the men were somewhat out of hand. They were mostly for 'drinking in alehouses' where the delinquents are sometimes 'taken by the vice-Chancellor, or for neglecting their studies or their Tutor's prayers.'"

[24] Sancroft refers to Dillingham's resignation from the Mastership of Emmanuel College in a letter dated 4 October 1662: "I was not heer a week before that Mastership of Eman. College became void by Dr Dillingham's recusancy to subscribe, and conform to the late Act of Uniformity ..." (Bodl. Tanner MS 48, f. 52).

[25] Shuckburgh, *Emmanuel College*, 103. On conscience, cf. Dillingham, *A Sermon at the Funeral of the Lady Elisabeth Alston* (London, 1678), 24-25: "But now a good Conscience, sprinkled with the Blood of Christ, that sincerely reports unto us, that we have by Faith in the Blood of Christ received him for the Pardon of Sin, and gives us an holy Life in evidence of the Truth of our Faith, doth thereby shew that the Promise of the Gospel, which was made conditionally is now become absolute unto us; and that therefore we are already passed from Death to Life...Thus we see that the Testimony of a good Conscience, (and nothing else without it) can give us true and solid Comfort, when we come to dy. ... An erroneous Conscience may make a man brave it out, and (with Curtius) leap desperately into the Gulf of the Bottomless Pit. An Hypocrite's Conscience may set a fair outside upon it, and dy (possibly) with seeming Joy; but in the midst of Laughter his Heart is sad."

[26] See R.E.C. Waters, *Genealogical Memoirs of the Extinct Family of Chester of Chicheley* (London, 1878), 639: "... I have sent my servant to cleare the lower study for your present use, according as you desire, untill such time as I can wait on you myselfe ... I have sent herewith my cope, and scarlet gown, and scarlet hood, and my surplice, about which I shall confer with you when we meet, and which you may please freely to make use of for your present occasions."

[27] Shuckburgh, *Emmanuel College*, 105.

connections with Emmanuel College would remain lifelong.[28] Dillingham spent the next ten years in retirement at Oundle. But it is a retirement characterized by literary and poetic activity.[29] 1672 saw the death of his wife, Elizabeth. In May of that year he was presented by his friend Sir Thomas Alston to the Rectory of Woodhill. The following year he married the thrice-widowed Mary Toller, who was fifty years of age according to the Isham correspondence,[30] and mother of seven children. He published in 1674 and 1675 respectively Thomas Horton's *Forty-six Sermons* and his *Choice and Practical Exposition on Four Select Psalms*. He also prepared for press Latin lives of Archbishop Ussher and Laurence Chaderton.[31] His last published poem (1680) was a brief neo-Latin epic entitled *Aegyptus Triumphata* on the plagues of Egypt. Two theological treatises were published just before his death in 1689. He was buried at Odell on 28 November 1689.

Such was the versatility of a seventeenth-century Anglo-Latin humanist most accurately described perhaps in Kelliher's phrase as an "entrepreneur of letters."[32] And it is to this entrepreneurship (especially as anthologist and neo-Latin poet) that we now turn.

Dillingham's literary entrepreneurship manifests itself most strikingly in his eagerness to make a wide and highly versatile range of neo-Latin poetry available to the wider world. In fact it was this that motivated several of his other literary projects even if these did not actually see the light of day. This was largely on account of his meticulous editorial care, evident in his practice of constant revision and the consistently scrupulous way in which he sought to obtain permission

---

[28] As late as 1678 he would describe to Sancroft his plan for converting the college chapel into a library: "... And I may give your Lordship an account also of Emmanuel library. I have observed the windows &c in the old chappel, and do not doubt but it may make a very convenient library, the walls are good and dry; the dampnes that appeares being only from the floore, which may be remedyed by raising the floore to the levell of the foot-pace of the Bachelors' Seates ..." (Odell 15 July 1678). (Bodl. MS Tanner 39, f. 65). Cited also at Waters, *Genealogical Memoirs*, 645.

[29] Two letters dated 14 February and 4 March 1671/2 respectively relate to the poetry of Justinian Isham, and allude to Dillingham's own translation into Latin of Herbert's "The Church Porch." Cf. *The Diary of Thomas Isham*, 82.

[30] *The Diary of Thomas Isham*, 82.

[31] These together with his exercises for the degrees of BD and DD (see BL Harley 7052) were published posthumously at Cambridge (1700) by his son Thomas.

[32] Kelliher, *ODNB* ad loc.

Introduction

from the contributors.[33] Extant among the manuscript holdings of the British Library are two unpublished neo-Latin anthologies compiled by Dillingham. The first of these is obviously incomplete. Entitled *Wilhelmi Dillinghami Poemata ab eo vel Inventa vel Versa vel aliunde adoptata et edita; quaedam nunc Primum ex ipsius Authoris Autographia*,[34] it runs to a mere seven folios, but even here is discernible once again that motivating breadth and diversity of subject matter. Thus biblical material (a Latin verse rendering [by David Pareus] of *Apoc.* 17),[35] is followed by John Hall's encomium of an anonymous author of gunpowder plot verses.[36] Royalist verses (to James I)[37] are followed by an incomplete Latin pastoral on the Gunpowder Plot.[38] The language, the genres, may be classical, but this is clearly a seventeenth-century world with its monarchs, and with plots against those monarchs as a Virgilian pastoral landscape is shattered and turned upside down by the sheer horror of a gunpowder conspiracy.

Much more extensive is Dillingham's unpublished *Poemata Selecta ex Autoribus qua Veteribus, qua Neotericis amplius Quadraginta fere non tam in vulgus nota; quaedam nunc primum edita*,[39] in which such Anglo-Latin poets as William Barclay, Giles Fletcher, and Thomas Masters are set alongside such continental authors as Beza and Natale Conti. While the range of authors falls far short of those eventually included in the published *Poemata Varii Argumenti*, the variety of subject matter is nonetheless impressive, embracing mathematics,[40] antiquarian

---

[33] Waters, *Genealogical Memoirs*, 640, correctly observes that Dillingham's literary projects "are most inadequately represented by his published works."

[34] BL Sloane 1815, ff 54-61.

[35] BL Sloane 1815, ff 55-56: *Prophetia ex Antiquiss. Cod. Mss in aedibus Praepositi Saleriani Reperto ad Missa David Pareus in cap. 17 Apocal* (1628).

[36] BL Sloane 1815, f. 57: *Versus Laudatorii J. Hall in auctorem cuiusdam carminis in coniurationem Sulphuream* (1605). Dillingham had himself composed laudatory English verses in praise of Hall's own poetry. These were included among the prefatory material to *Poems by John Hall* (Cambridge, 1646).

[37] BL Sloane 1815, ff 58-58^v: *Versus Heroici Ad Regem [Iacobum I] inscripti et carmine supradicto praefixi*.

[38] BL Sloane 1815, ff 59-61: *Carmen in Coniurationem Sulphuream* [Imperfect].

[39] BL Sloane 1766.

[40] William Barclay, *Arithmeticae Memorativae* (BL Sloane 1766, ff 15-21).

matters,[41] monastic life,[42] hunting,[43] and even the game of shovel-board.[44] The multiple aims of this literary project were articulated by Dillingham in an insightful letter (to his lifelong friend and critic William Sancroft) dated 18 September 1671,[45] and can be seen to encapsulate a sense of vocation that inspired his literary ambitions in general:

> [My small Designe of a collection of poems] ... therefore shall now more fully acquaint you with what I propounded to my selfe in undertaking it. Which was to make a collection of such poems as for variety of matter and elegancy of verse might be profitable and delightfull to scholars of all conditions; and in so doing to revive some pieces of worth yet not like otherwise to be reprinted; to communicate others which are *non tam in vulgus nota*; to collect some which lay dispersed, and to publish others not yet printed. In the whole I have regard to the delicacy of the present age by making choice only of Such as have clearnese and facility of expression.[46]

The statement reveals a fourfold aim: of variety, pleasure, practical usefulness, and making accessible to a wide audience poetry hitherto unknown—all attuned to suit "the delicacy of the present age."

In many respects Dillingham's peculiarly modern vision combined with his lateral thinking helped to pave the way for a range of subsequent neo-Latin anthologies that would be published in England in the seventeenth and eighteenth centuries. Foremost among these are Francis Atterbury's ’Ανθολογία (1684),[47] which would be revised and expanded in 1740 by Alexander Pope as *Selecta Poemata Italorum*.[48] But the

---

[41] Giles Fletcher, *De Literis Antiquae Britanniae* (BL Sloane 1766, ff 34-42).

[42] Laelius Capilupus, *De Vita Monachorum* (BL Sloane 1766, ff 204-211).

[43] Natale Conti, *De Venatione* (BL Sloane 1766, ff 270-277).

[44] Thomas Masters, *Mensa Lubrica* (BL Sloane 1766, ff 289-290).

[45] David Money, *The English Horace: Anthony Alsop and the Tradition of British Latin Verse* (Oxford, 1998), 40, incorrectly assumes that this letter describes the *Poemata Varii Argumenti*. It is clear from Dillingham's stated intention to include in the anthology Conti's *De Venatione* that the letter alludes in fact to the unpublished *Poemata Selecta* (BL Sloane 1766), in which that precise work occurs at ff 270-277. Conti's poem is not anthologized in Dillingham's published *Poemata Varii Argumenti*.

[46] Bodl. MS Tanner 44, f. 274.

[47] ’Ανθολογία seu Selecta Quaedam Poemata Italorum qui Latine Scripserunt (London, 1684).

Anglo-Latin dimension is perhaps best epitomized by the *Musae Anglicanae* compiled at the end of the seventeenth century by Joseph Addison[49] and revised and augmented in the following century by Vincent Bourne.[50] It is hardly a coincidence that Bourne's anthology would include Dillingham's original Latin compositions.[51]

Returning to the *Poemata Varii Argumenti*, evidence would suggest that Dillingham took no small pride in his own quite substantial contribution to that anthology. Writing to Sancroft in October 1677, he wonders about the title of the collection: should he simply call the volume *Herberti Poemata Quaedam, Latine Reddita &c.* even though his versions of Herbert comprise only one quarter of the whole? Should the work perhaps fall "under the title of mine, which wilbe with them, about halfe the Book"? Should he have "some more general title to comprehend all in one"?[52] Sancroft seems to have suggested a compromise, which is quite likely reflected in the title eventually chosen,[53] even if that title is in

---

[48] *Selecta Poemata Italorum qui Latine Scripserunt, cura cuiusdam Anonymi Anno 1684 Congesta, Iterum in Lucem Data, Una Cum Aliorum Italorum Operibus, Accurante A. Pope* (London, 1740), 2 vols.

[49] *Musarum Anglicanarum Analecta* (Oxford, 1699).

[50] Vincent Bourne, ed. *Musarum Anglicanarum Analecta* (London, 1741), 2 vols. Bourne moves beyond Addison by including Cambridge as well as Oxford neo-Latin poets.

[51] Bourne includes Dillingham's *Suleianum* and *Campanae Undellenses* at *Musarum Anglicanarum Analecta*, I, 109-112 and 244-248 respectively. See Estelle Haan, *Classical Romantic: Identity in the Latin Poetry of Vincent Bourne* (Transactions of the American Philosophical Society 97.1 [Philadelphia, 2007]), 10.

[52] Bodl. MS Tanner 40, f. 109 (22 October 1677) [Dillingham to Sancroft]: "... Also I begg your advice whether I should make the Title *Herberti Poemata quaedam, Latine reddita &c* (which are but a 4th of the booke) which will be most known, and seemly due to his name; or whether Under the title of mine, which wilbe, with them, about halfe of the Booke. Or else under some more general title to comprehend all in one. Among them there are versions of severall parts of Scripture by Grotius, Thuanus, and others; and some short papers of those which you formerly saw from Mr Hookes hand."

[53] Sancroft replied thus in a letter included in BL Sloane 1710, f. 212: "For the Title, I would sett it, as in the inclosed." His enclosure does not survive. Given, however, the readiness with which Dillingham elsewhere heeded Sancroft's advice in regard to his literary projects in general and his Latin poetry in particular, it is probably reasonable to assume that the present title is that suggested by Sancroft in that now lost enclosure.

fact rather misleading in that it fails to take account of the sheer range of Part Two. Misleading though it may be, it is a title that confidently and quite self-consciously juxtaposes two Cambridge poets: George Herbert and William Dillingham. The juxtaposition is a felicitous one for in the first part of this volume vernacular poetry is now recast and amplified via Latin verse paraphrase, which in turn is complemented by original neo-Latin poetry.

Indeed if the composition of Latin poetry enabled an author to take his place alongside neo-Latin writers in England and on the continent, so too was translation into Latin regarded as a means of explicating, augmenting, and enhancing a vernacular original. The preface to Dillingham's edition (1653) of Theodore Bathurst's Latin version of Spenser's *The Shepheardes Calendar* is permeated by positive imagery of resurrection and revitalization: Spenser, now clad in a Roman toga (*indutus idem Romana toga*),[54] seems not so much to have been "translated" as to have been "restored."[55] But more than that: Bathurst's Latin version can illuminate, facilitate, and even embellish the original English.[56] The same can be said to be true of Dillingham's Latin renderings of Herbert's English poetry. These are the poems with which the *Poemata Varii Argumenti* open. In his introductory preface (*Ad Lectorem*) Dillingham takes pains to point out that his free version (*versio libera*) of Herbert is intended both to illuminate obscurities inherent in the original vernacular and to expand upon the *sententia auctoris*:

> Quocirca nonnulla ex iis seligenda duxi, quae versione libera ita demum Latine redderem, ut et obscuris lumen aliquod afferrem, et sententiam Auctoris alicubi dilatarem.[57]

---

[54] *Calendarium Pastorale sive Aeglogae Duodecim, Totidem Anni Mensibus Accommodatae. Anglice olim Scriptae ab Edmundo Spensero Anglorum Poetarum Principe: Nunc autem Eleganti Latino carmine donatae a Theodoro Bathurst* (London, 1653), A3ᵛ: *erat olim tibi Spenserus tuus in deliciis; quocirca nullus metuo ne ingratus hodie tibi sit, indutus idem Romana toga; quae ita quidem illum decet, tamque apte ille convenit, ut non alia cute natus, aut in eam non tam translatus, quam restitutus esse videatur* (Prefatory epistle to Francis Lane).

[55] *Calendarium Pastorale*, A3ᵛ: *non tam translatus, quam restitutus esse videatur.*

[56] *Calendarium Pastorale*, A4ʳ: *et quidem ita vertit, ut et obscuris lucem et facilitatem asperis atque omnibus nitorem ac elegantiam foeneraverit.*

[57] *Poemata Varii Argumenti*, A2ᵛ.

Introduction

This twofold methodological aim is likewise acknowledged in Dillingham's letter to Sancroft dated 19 June 1676, in which he alludes to his Latin verse rendering of Herbert's "The Church-Porch," included in papers that have

> attempted not to rebuild a Church (that is a work worthy of you) but to translate a churchporch wherein yet I have not confined my selfe to the laws of a translation, but have taken to my selfe more liberty (especially in some places) of explaining and adding as you will easily perceive if you take but the English along with you in the perusal.[58]

In his reply Sancroft describes the version as an "excellently-well-labor'd Translation," remarking that, given the obscurities inherent in the original vernacular, it would be unreasonable to expect a verse for verse rendering.[59] In his view Dillingham's version is to be regarded as a "paraphrase" employing "liberty," a work that can "be at once Translation and Comment too."[60] Central to such "commentary" are the "additions" which, says Sancroft, enrich Herbert's poem while demonstrating Dillingham's originality.[61] He conveys this via a spring/river metaphor:

> Had I not been convinced of it before, I should from hence have collected how much better any Author (—*pretium cui Vena facit*) writes from his own living Spring, than from anothers River, flow it never so rich or so clear.[62]

A Latin rendering should thus function not as a verbatim translation, but essentially as an illuminating means of exhibiting originality and inventiveness. Or in the words of the translation theorist Eugene Nida:

---

[58] Bodl. MS Tanner 40, f. 7 (dated 19 June 1676).

[59] "But the next Return brought me something farr more welcome, your excellently-well-labor'd Translation of Mr Herbert's Porch. It were unreasonable to expect you should measure Verse for Verse from an Author that writes so very close; I might add (in consequence) so obscure too" (BL Sloane 1710, f. 206).

[60] "And therefore your paraphrase, where you have us'd your Liberty, will oblige your Readers, and be at once Translation and Comment too" (BL Sloane 1710, f. 206).

[61] "And then for your Additions, they are so good, and so suited to your Text, they so enrich that who so considers them will say they are or ought to be there" (BL Sloane 1710, f. 206).

[62] BL Sloane 1710, f. 206.

> [The translator] must understand not only the obvious content of the message, but also the subtleties of meaning, the significant emotive values of words and the stylistic features which determine the "flavor and feel" of the message. ... In other words, in addition to a knowledge of the two or more languages involved in the translational process, the translator must have a thorough acquaintance with the subject matter concerned.[63]

Nida proceeds to argue that the translator should admire the author, have the same cultural background, the same talent, and should present the same joy to the reader that is given by the original.

The "joy" that can derive from such inventiveness is regarded by Dillingham as fundamental to both the translating and the reading processes. The ideal methodology is to read a vernacular and its Latin version side by side and *pari passu*. This is apparent from one of Dillingham's letters to Sancroft in 1676. Commenting on the latter's Latin version of John Denham's vernacular poem "Cooper's Hill," he regrets that he did not have the English to hand when critiquing Sancroft's Latin rendering and was thereby deprived of the delight that would accrue from observing "the harmony between the translation and the original" of a work that "may passe for a native of old Rome were not the subject modern."[64]

But while Dillingham played an important role in the transmission of Herbert's English poetry (and is thought to have owned the manuscript of the latter's *Musae Responsoriae*),[65] he was also a significantly accomplished neo-Latin poet in his own right, possessed of his own

---

[63] E.A. Nida, *Toward a Science of Translating: With Special Reference to Principles and Procedures Involved in Bible Translating* (Leiden, 1964), 150-151. On translation theory, see among others L.G. Kelly, *The True Interpreter: A History of Translation Theory and Practice in the West* (Oxford, 1979); Rainer Schulte and John Biguenet, eds., *Theories of Translation: An Anthology of Essays from Dryden to Derrida* (Chicago, 1992); Edwin Gentzler, *Contemporary Translation Theories* (London and New York, 1993); Cecil Hargreaves, *A Translator's Freedom: Modern English Bibles and Their Language* (Sheffield, 1993).

[64] Bodl. MS Tanner 40, f. 14: "I here returne you the poem of Cowpers hill which I have perused with great delight and can not but think it excellent in itselfe, though having never seen that which it translates, I must needs want much of the delight which I presume would arise from the harmony between the translation and the original. But as it is, it may passe for a native of old Rome were not the subject modern" (Dated July 1676).

[65] The Latin preface to James Duport's *Ecclesiastes Solomonis* (Cambridge, 1662), 6ʳ, states that it was from Dillingham that Duport obtained the manuscript of Herbert's *Musae Responsoriae*. See Elizabeth Clark, "George Herbert and Cambridge Scholars," *George Herbert Journal* 27 (2006), 43-52, at 48-49.

"living spring," so to speak. And it is in this latter capacity that his work has been either entirely overlooked or at best dismissed in a rather cavalier fashion by critics and commentators. All too frequently his original Latin verse has been regarded as no more than a pastime, a pleasurable activity undertaken by a poet in rustic retirement at Oundle. Waters, for example, describes it in terms couched in a quasi-romantic subjectivity as "the favourite amusement of his leisure,"[66] seeing his talent "in criticism rather than in original composition,"[67] while offering the surely blinkered viewpoint that "his verses have a certain second-rate merit, but seldom rise above the level of University prize poems."[68] It is a criticism that seems to have stuck. Thus more recently Kelliher's otherwise excellent account of the poet seems to follow suit in describing him as "amusing himself by writing verses in English and Latin which he shared with his friends."[69] Perhaps it is the superficial simplicity of such verse that has led to this blighted view, a view that is very much at odds with the laudatory terms in which Sancroft refers to Dillingham's Latin poetry. And such praise cannot be neatly explained away by the fact that the two men were close friends.[70] Likewise his debt to the poets of classical Rome has been underplayed. Bradner has remarked that the subjects of Dillingham's Latin verse "show his complete independence of the old school of classical imitation."[71] While it is undeniable that such topics as sporting on a seventeenth-century bowling green, the tolling of church bells at night, the flight of a fledgling bird, or the beauties of a garden hedge seem to locate that verse in a world far removed from things classical, Bradner's comment requires qualification and

---

[66] "The favourite amusement of his leisure was in the composition of verses in Latin and English, for which he had a marvellous facility" (Waters, *Genealogical Memoirs*, 641).

[67] "His talent lay in criticism rather than in original composition, and he makes a better figure in other men's books than in his own" (Waters, *Genealogical Memoirs*, 640).

[68] Waters, *Genealogical Memoirs*, 641.

[69] Kelliher, *ODNB* ad loc.

[70] Waters, *Genealogical Memoirs*, 643, presents the rather blinkered viewpoint that Sancroft's letters to Dillingham "do more credit to the Archbishop's affection for his friend than to his critical taste."

[71] Leicester Bradner, *Musae Anglicanae: A History of Anglo-Latin Poetry 1500-1925* (London and New York, 1940), 204.

modification in that it overlooks a key aspect of Dillingham's methodology. Central to that methodology is the way in which the poems engage with a wide range of classical intertexts, for now in fact it is as though Dillingham's own Latin verse "may passe for a native of old Rome were not the subject modern."[72] For, as Hale has remarked, neo-Latin literature is perhaps the most intertextual of forms.[73] Indeed in many respects the nature and style of Dillingham's Latin poetry foreshadow (and to some degree inspired) that fusion of the classical and the romantic so central to Vincent Bourne's Latin verse.[74]

Bradner was also of the viewpoint that the pieces in Part Two of the *Poemata Varii Argumenti* were included "without any guiding principle of selection."[75] Money, by contrast, while not illustrating the point, has stated that Dillingham's methodological practice was "not quite haphazard."[76] And this can be taken one stage further. In several respects the range of neo-Latin verse selected by Dillingham for inclusion in Part Two serves to complement several of his own original Latin poems appearing in Part One. Thus the genre of the sports-poem exemplified by Dillingham's *Suleianum* (on a game of bowls) is represented on a more extensive level by Vida's *Scacchia Ludus* (on the game of chess),[77] a work that in many respects constitutes the father of this neo-Latin genre. Likewise Dillingham's *Avicula*, depicting a fledgling bird receiving instruction from her mother in the art of flying, is complemented by three bird-poems in Part Two: Bartassius's *De Aquila* (which describes inter alia eaglets in their nest awaiting food from their mother and exposed to a variety of dangers),[78] the same author's verses

---

[72] See note 64 above.

[73] J.K. Hale, *Milton's Languages: The Impact of Multilingualism on Style* (Cambridge, 1997), 12: "[Intertextuality] is precisely the aspect of neo-Latin poetry which deters and baffles us, because the degree of verbal allusiveness to the ancients either seems servile or vanishes in translation. It is time that literary theory rescued it, as being the most intertextual poetry known to Europe."

[74] See Haan, *Classical Romantic: Identity in the Latin Poetry of Vincent Bourne*, passim.

[75] Bradner, *Musae Anglicanae*, 205.

[76] Money, *The English Horace*, 40.

[77] *Poemata Varii Argumenti*, 134-154.

[78] *Bartassius De Aquila, Gabr. Lermaeo Interprete* (*Poemata Varii Argumenti*, 160-162).

on the nightingale (*De Luscinia*)[79] and Strada's Latin fable on a contest between a nightingale and a musician.[80] Dillingham's garden topiary (*Sepes Hortensis*) finds a companion piece of sorts in the pseudo-Virgilian *Moretum* describing the abundance of a *hortus*.[81] And even the quasi-moralistic *Nemesis a Tergo* (highlighting the inevitability of retribution for wrongdoing) can profitably be viewed alongside the extract from Manilius's *Astronomicon* 5 now appearing under the title *Perseus Vindex*.[82] In other words it could be argued that the collection as a whole serves to showcase in a variety of ways Dillingham's original Latin poetry presented for the first time in a much wider neo-Latin and classical context.

This brief study will focus on Dillingham's original Latin verse contributions to the *Poemata Varii Argumenti*. It will do so in an attempt to disprove two claims: 1) that Dillingham's talent lay in criticism rather than in original composition (Waters); 2) that his Latin poetry shows his complete independence of the old school of classical imitation (Bradner). It has the twofold aim of highlighting both the classical and the contemporary intertexts with which this hitherto neglected poetry engages. It will argue that far from constituting the leisurely product of a gentleman in rustic retirement, this is highly talented verse that "sports" with the classics in several ways: first in its self-consciously playful interaction with the Latin poets of Augustan Rome, chiefly Virgil and Ovid; second in its appropriation of a classical world and its linguistic medium to describe such seventeenth-century sports or pastimes as bowling, horticulture, and bell-ringing. It will also foreground the pseudoromanticism surprisingly inherent in the work of a late-seventeenth-century poet, who, it will be argued, discovered in his twilight years a neo-Latin inspirational Muse.

---

[79] *Idem de Luscinia, eodem Interprete* (*Poemata Varii Argumenti*, 163-164).

[80] *Fam. Strada de Luscinia et Fidicine* (*Poemata Varii Argumenti*, 165-166).

[81] *P. Virgilii Maronis (ut vulgo habetur) Moretum* (*Poemata Varii Argumenti*, 120-124).

[82] *M. Manilii Perseus Vindex e Lib. V Astron.* (*Poemata Varii Argumenti*, 131-133).

Chapter 1

Sporting with the Classics: *Suleianum*

Suleianum takes as its subject the sport of bowling. That the sport was a popular pastime in seventeenth-century England is attested by, for example, the Diary of John Evelyn[1] or such works as Robert Howlett's *The School of Recreation* (1696).[2] Dillingham's bowling-match, however, is recreated not in vernacular prose, but in Latin verse. The choice of linguistic medium can only serve to enhance the mock-epic qualities of a poem that reinvents and appropriates a classical world to a seventeenth-century setting. And it does so on a generic as well as a topographical level. For while, as noted below, the poem looks back to classical precedent, and especially to the games of Virgil, *Aeneid* 5,[3] it also assumes a place within a miniature neo-Latin genre that had already begun to come to prominence in the Renaissance: the Latin verse-description of sports and pastimes. Furthermore, it may have helped to inaugurate in England a neo-Latin and vernacular tradition of bowling-green verse, in which the classical and the contemporary are juxtaposed and reconciled albeit in rather different ways.

As Bradner has noted, the hallmark of the neo-Latin sports poem is its skillful presentation of a familiar object or pastime in a strange

---

[1] Cf. *John Evelyn: Diary*, ed. E.S. De Beer (Oxford, 1955), III, 68: "11 June 1652 About 4 in the afternoone, beeing at bowles on the Greene;" *Diary*, III, 219: "14 Aug 1658 We went to a challeng'd match to Durdens to Bowles for 10 pounds, which we wonn." Cf. Joseph Addison, *Spectator*, 126 (25 July 1711) in *The Spectator*, ed. D.F. Bond (Oxford, 1965), II, 3-4: "Being upon the Bowling-green at a neighbouring market town the other day (for that is the place where the gentlemen of one side meet once a week)."

[2] Robert Howlett, *The School of Recreation, or, A Guide to the Most Ingenious Exercises of Hunting, Riding, Racing, Fireworks, Military Discipline, The Science of Defence, Hawking, Tennis, Bowling, Ringing, Singing, Cock-Fighting, Fowling* (London, 1698), 95-96.

[3] See 31-37 below.

setting.[4] It is a genre represented (even if rather sporadically) by several seventeenth-century Anglo-Latin poets. Thus at the close of that century Joseph Addison was able to include in his *Musae Anglicanae*[5] neo-Latin poems on such activities as bullbaiting,[6] cockfighting,[7] and skating,[8] while in the following century Latin poems on handball and football were anthologized by Edward Popham in his *Selecta Poemata Anglorum Latina* (1774).[9] Although some are obviously more successful than others, all are united in their appropriation of the language of classical Rome to describe various sporting activities in a contemporary English setting. They are moreover characterized by the mock-epic heroism in which the seemingly trivial is enshrouded. Perhaps most strikingly Addison's Latin poem *Sphaeristerium* takes bowls as its subject, not without a backward glance at Dillingham's piece,[10] which directly preceded it in the pirated *Examen Poeticum Duplex* (1698).[11] Both works may owe some debt to Thomas Masters's *Mensa Lubrica* (1658), a Latin poem on the Shovel Board[12] (the ancestor of the modern American game of shuffle board), significantly anthologized by Dillingham in his projected though

---

[4] Bradner, *Musae Anglicanae*, 221.

[5] On Addison's anthology and on his own neo-Latin verse contributions to the same, see Estelle Haan, *Vergilius Redivivus: Studies in Joseph Addison's Latin Poetry* (Transactions of the American Philosophical Society 95.2 [Philadelphia, 2005]), passim.

[6] Francis Knapp, *Taurus in Circo* (*Musae Anglicanae* II, 80-84).

[7] Joseph Friend, *Pugna Gallorum Gallinaceorum* (*Musae Anglicanae* II, 85-90).

[8] Philip Frowde, *Cursus Glacialis* (*Musae Anglicanae* II, 145-147).

[9] See Arthur Bedford, *Lusus Pilae Palmariae* and Anon., *Pila Pedalis* in *Selecta Poemata Anglorum, Seu Sparsim Edita, Seu Hactenus Inedita*, ed. Edward Popham (Bath, 1774-1776), I, 43-47 and 82-84.

[10] See Haan, *Vergilius Redivivus: Studies in Joseph Addison's Latin Poetry*, 94-103.

[11] *Examen Poeticum Duplex* (London, 1698), 29-33. Dillingham's poem was not anthologized by Addison in the *Musae Anglicanae*, which was based on the output of Oxford poets.

[12] *Musae Anglicanae* I, 17-19. Bradner, *Musae Anglicanae*, 204, overstates the question of "influence" by asserting that Dillingham's poem "was probably inspired" by Masters's piece, and that "either he [Dillingham] or Masters was, in turn, the cause of Addison's later *Sphaeristerium*." On possible points of contact, however, between Masters and Dillingham and between Masters and Addison, see Haan, *Vergilius Redivivus: Studies in Joseph Addison's Latin Poetry*, 93-103.

unpublished *Poemata Selecta*.[13] But it was the game of bowling in particular that would function, and perhaps surprisingly so, as an inspirational muse for subsequent vernacular and neo-Latin poets. Francis Quarles, for example, extols the sport in English verses included by Robert Howlett in his description of bowling in *The School of Recreation* (1698).[14] And the trend continued into the eighteenth century exemplified perhaps most notably by William Somervile's "The Bowling-Green" (1727),[15] the neo-Latin *Sphaeromachia: Anglice Bowling* (1743) "by a gentleman, late of Balliol College, Oxford",[16] John Marchant's "The Bowling-Green Or Trade Fortuitous" (1753),[17] and Samuel Bentley, "The Bowling-Green" (1774).[18] In this later tradition the very sport of bowling can hold a mirror up to society and humankind in general. For Marchant it functions as an allegory of commercial enterprise: "thus Trade may be termed the Green,"[19] while for Richard Seymour it is "the Emblem of the World."[20]

But if we are to trace the father of this miniature genre it is to sixteenth-century Italy that we must turn. Marco Girolamo Vida's

---

[13] See *Poemata Selecta ex Auctoribus qua Veteribus, qua Neotericis Amplius Quadraginta* (BL Sloane 1766), ff 289-290 = *Thomae Mastersii Oxoniensis Mensa Lubrica*.

[14] Robert Howlett, *The School of Recreation*, 96.

[15] William Somervile, "The Bowling Green," *Occasional Poems, Translations, Fables, Tales &c.* (London, 1727), 67-80.

[16] See William Major, *Four Satires Translated from the Latin into English Verse. To which are Added Some Occasional Poems on Various Subjects by a Gentleman, Late of Balliol College, Oxford* (London, 1743), 78-80.

[17] John Marchant, *Lusus Iuveniles or Youth's Recreation* (London, 1753), 53-55.

[18] Samuel Bentley, *Poems on Various Occasions: Consisting of Original Pieces and Translations* (London, 1774), 131-159.

[19] See John Marchant, "The Bowling Green," 41-44: "Thus Trade may be termed the Green,/And Profit the Jack that is thrown;/The Tradesmen and Merchants are keen,/All trying to make it their own."

[20] Richard Seymour, *The Compleat Gamester* (London, 1739), 324: "To give you the Moral of it, it is the Emblem of the World, or of the World's Ambition, where most are short, over-wide or wrong byassed, and some few justle into the Favour of Mrs Fortune and with Her it is, as in the Court, where the nearest are the most spighted, and all Bowls aim at the other."

Scacchia Ludus (1525)[21] had described in highly Virgilian language a chess game by Apollo and Mercury played in the presence of the other gods. Vida's poem was very well known in England from the late sixteenth century onwards, and was actually anthologized by Dillingham in the second part of the *Poemata Varii Argumenti* (1678) as if to complement his own bowling poem.[22] There is evidence to suggest, moreover, that it had already made a not insignificant impact upon such neo-Latin poets as Thomas Watson, whose *Amintae Gaudia* (London, 1592), included as *Eclogue* 6 a battle between Jupiter and Pluto, and introduced the whole by the gift of a chess set, with the battle itself depicted in terms of the movements on a chessboard.[23] Crucially, the neo-Latin sports poem provided such eighteenth-century vernacular writers as Alexander Pope with the germ and the paragon of the mock-epic battle most skillfully epitomized perhaps by the card game brilliantly described in the *Rape of the Lock* III.[24] Something of this generic awareness can be seen to underlie Samuel Bentley's rather self-conscious statement concerning his so-called disassociation from neo-Latin precedent. Speaking of his vernacular poem "The Bowling-Green," he proclaims:

> The Bowling-Green is one of the latest productions; and how the Public may be pleased with the versification, the conduct, and mechanical parts of it, I cannot pretend to say: but as I think very little has been written upon the subject, it will be found, at least, to be an original: very little of the machinery of antiquity made use of by Vida in his *Schaccia* [sic], could be introduced into it; nor could much be gathered from Mr. Addison, who only gives us the outlines of the diversion of the Bowling-Green in his *Sphaeristerium*.[25]

---

[21] See *The Game of Chess: Marco Girolamo Vida's Scacchia Ludus*, ed. with introduction and notes by M.A. Di Cesare (*Bibliotheca Humanistica & Reformatorica* 13: Nieuwkoop, 1975).

[22] *Poemata Varii Argumenti*, 134-154. On the rather self-conscious interrelationship between Parts One and Two of the *Poemata Varii Argumenti*, see 14-15 above.

[23] Cf. Bradner, *Musae Anglicanae*, 48. Cf. E.R. Bulwer Lytton, "The Chess Board," which fuses the mock-heroic and the amatory: "When you and I played chess together,/Checkmated by each other's eyes./Ah, still I see your soft white hand/Hovering warm o'er Queen and Knight./Brave Pawns in valiant battle stand:/The double Castles guard the wings:/The Bishop, bent on distant things,/Moves, sidling, through the fight" (5-12). Text is that of R.M. Leonard, ed., *A Book of Light Verse* (Oxford and London, 1910), 147.

[24] See in general George de Forest Lord, *Heroic Mockery: Variations on Epic Themes From Homer to Joyce* (New Jersey, 1977), 27-58.

[25] Samuel Bentley, *Poems on Various Occasions*, xvii-xviii (Preface).

That Bentley feels the need to make such an *apologia*, as it were, is significant. And we can read between the lines: the sports-poem, whether in Latin or English, *was* expected to implement the "machinery of antiquity,"[26] a methodology epitomized in Italy and England by Vida and Addison respectively. In fact Bentley's associated claim to originality falls rather flat as does his dismissal of Addison's treatment of the subject of bowls. Whether he knew of Dillingham's Latin poem remains unknown.

The *Suleianum*, like the majority of Dillingham's original Latin verse, can be dated to the 1680s when he was living in pseudoretirement at Oundle, a period during which he shared such poetry with his friends and acquaintances. And this is particularly pertinent in this instance. Included among his unpublished poetic anthology *Poemata Selecta* is an anonymous Latin poem entitled *Sphaeristerium*,[27] which likewise takes bowling as its subject and was composed at Oundle. Signed "This for his reverend friend, Dr Dillingham at Oundale," this quasi-Ovidian Latin piece is cast in elegiacs as opposed to hexameters, the traditional meter of the neo-Latin sports poem. While the respective chronology of, and relationship between, this poem and *Suleianum* may be impossible to determine with any degree of accuracy (although it is tempting to regard it as a response to Dillingham's piece), it is interesting to note that it likewise eroticizes the role of the jack, albeit on a much more extensive level, depicting it as a second Penelope, about whom swarm a multitude of suitors, the bowls themselves. While transporting the whole to Ithaca, this rather skillful poem transforms the archery competition set by Penelope for her suitors[28] into a bowling match not entirely dissimilar to that depicted in *Suleianum*. Indeed, as noted below, there are some further links between the two poems as, like the bowlers themselves, one poet seems to strive to outdo his opponent. As such Dillingham's piece takes its place within, and engages with, a complex intertextual network.

---

[26] Despite this disclaimer, as it were, Bentley in the poem proper invokes the Muse "Who taught the bards of old in lofty strains,/To sing heroical Olympic plains;/The noble champions bidding them rehearse,/And praise the victors in immortal verse:/And in their songs made rapid chariots roll,/In swift contention for the distant goal" (Samuel Bentley, "The Bowling-Green," *Poems on Various Occasions*, 132, lines 1-6).

[27] *Poemata Selecta ex Autoribus qua Veteribus, qua Neotericis amplius Quadraginta fere non tam in vulgus nota; quaedam nunc primum edita* (BL Sloane 1766, ff 328-329^v).

[28] See Homer, *Odyssey* 21. 75-77.

Suleianum is addressed to Charles Fane (1635-1691), third Earl of Westmorland.[29] The bowling green upon which this neo-Latin game is played is that of the Earl's residence at Sulehay Lodge[30] to the west of Oundle and eight miles west of Peterborough. Bradner regards this "definite local setting" as rendering the piece more pleasing than the comparable poems by Masters and Addison,[31] a viewpoint surely open to question. Addison's poem in particular is a highly skillful piece especially in terms of its engagement with the Virgilian poetic corpus.[32]

Situated on a raised level with a prospect of valleys and fields below and beside a bridge and stream,[33] the setting of Dillingham's match (and hence of the poem) conforms to the ideal location for a bowling green as recommended by Samuel Bentley, who proclaims:

> Let distant prospects open to the sight
> Let it not low, or in a bottom lie,
> Nor yet its elevation be too high;
> Between the two extremes with nicest care,
> And with exactness form the oblong square.[34]

He advocates that the site be neither too low nor too high,[35] but that it should constitute a rustic, rural setting of surrounding fields, trees and

---

[29] *Ad Illustrissimum Carolum Westmorliandiae Comitem.*

[30] Sulehay Lodge was presented to Catherine Howard by Henry VIII (as part of her wedding gift). Little of that dwelling survives. The present house was constructed on the site of the original stables.

[31] Bradner, *Musae Anglicanae*, 204.

[32] See Haan, *Vergilius Redivivus: Studies in Joseph Addison's Latin Poetry*, 88-103.

[33] Cf. *Suleianum* 1-5: *Aufonias propter ripas, qua cogitur unda/ferre iugum et famam debet Wansfordia ponti,/silvae contiguus modicique cacumine montis/est locus Australem qui partem versus et ortum/vallesque villasque et longos prospicit agros.*

[34] Samuel Bentley, "The Bowling Green," *Poems on Various Occasions*, 133, lines 2-6. Bentley's lines may look back to Virgil's prescriptive account of the site of the beehive in *Georgics* 4.8-24.

[35] Cf. Charles Cotton, *The Compleat Gamester: Or Full and Easy Instruction for Playing at Above Twenty Several Games Upon the Cards* (London, 1726), 222: Ch. V: "Of Bowling": "In Bowling there is a great Art in chusing out the Ground, and preventing the Windings, Hanging and many turning Advantages of the same, whether it be in open wide Places, as Bares, and Bowling-greens, or in close Bowling-Alleys."

streams.[36] Likewise William Somervile locates his bowling-match "where fair Sabrina's wand'ring currents flow/A large smooth Plain extends its verdant brow."[37] In Dillingham, the location (*est locus* [4])[38] is depicted as a quasi-pastoral *locus amoenus* possessed of its own river, woodland, perspective, and shade. Significantly, however, it is a *locus amoenus* with a difference. In the punning phrase *Aufonias ... ripas* (1) the world of Ausonian pastoral has been transported to England, transformed as it now is into the banks of the river Avon, while the traditional shade afforded the shepherd by trees[39] has become the clubhouse, the *gratissima fessis/umbra viris* (27-28), from which the *puer* retrieves, and in which he stores the bowls as though he were penning his sheep in their fold.[40] Likewise the shepherds of classical pastoral have been replaced, if not to some degree displaced, by the nobility, a *generosa cohors* (14).[41]

---

[36] Samuel Bentley, "The Bowling Green," *Poems on Various Occasions*, 133, lines 9-12: "Let lofty trees in proper places rise,/To screen the ground-plot from inclement skies:/Trees from the cold, and blighting winds defend;/And from too scorching heats a shelter lend." Cf. Samuel Bentley, "The Bowling Green," *Poems on Various Occasions*, 135, line 20–136, lines 1-2: "Yonder clear fountain can a stream supply,/In pleasing murmurs o'er the pebbles glide,/And in meanders round its passage guide."

[37] William Somervile, "The Bowling Green," 1-2.

[38] Cf. Anon., *Sphaeromachia* 4: *hic locus est*.

[39] Cf., for example, Virgil, *Ecl.* 1.1: *Tityre, tu patulae recubans sub tegmine fagi*; *Ecl.* 1.4: *tu, Tityre, lentus in umbra*. All quotations are from *The Eclogues of Vergil*, ed. Robert Coleman (Cambridge, 1977). Cf. Addison, *Sphaeristerium* 65-66: *lenia iam zephyri spirantes frigora et umbrae/captantur, vultuque fluens abstergitur umor*.

[40] *hinc puer expromit sphaeras, hic nocte recondit* (29). The quasi-pastoral subtext is highlighted by an anonymous translator of the poem, who reworks this line as "This is the place, wherein the boy doth keep/By night, as in a field, his wooden sheep" (38-39). See Bodl. MS. Eng. Misc. d.1, ff 45-47, at f. 45, and Appendix 2 below.

[41] In Dillingham's poem bowling functions for the nobility as a means of dispelling cares (*generosa cohors animo depellere curas/quum iuvat* [14-15]). Cf. Masters, *Mensa Lubrica* 4: *ubi sepositis placuerunt otia curis*. Pope, *Rape of the Lock* 3.9-10: "Hither the Heroes and the Nymphs resort,/To taste awhile the Pleasures of a Court." Text is that of *Alexander Pope: The Rape of the Lock*, ed. Cythia Wall (Boston and New York, 1998). On bowling as a game reserved for the upper classes, cf. the highlighting in the Anon., *Sphaeromachia* that the competitors constitute *Armigerique Equitesque* (5) and the associated injunction that the common people betake themselves afar: *vos, o vulgares animi, procul este profani;/accipiat nullas tali Plebecula sorores* (7-8), itself a parodic echo of the injunction uttered by classical priests and priestesses, urging the uninitiated to steer clear of a religious

In fact that "pleasing" quality highlighted by Bradner manifests itself in the poem in a variety of ways: in, for example, the stunned reaction of the natural world to a lawn roller or to the frantic fervor, antics and activities of impassioned competitors in the match itself; in the personification of the jack as a female whose magnetism, so to speak, attracts the bowls themselves, and who wins the admiration and veneration of the bowling and indeed bowing participants; in the mock-heroic grandeur of a sport that becomes an epic battle of sorts; in the homely realistic description of aspects of the sport itself: the comparative weight of the bowls, the rest afforded by the clubhouse, the physical contortions of the players as each urges his bowl along the green; in the evocation of a range of classical games via an explicit simile, and also intertextually in terms of the piece's interaction with *Aeneid* 5.

Hand in hand with the poem's inherent pastoralism is Dillingham's presentation of the pristine innocence of the landscape before it was leveled into a bowling green. This is conveyed in language (*terra olim agricolae duros experta labores* [6])[42] evocative of the world of Virgil's *Georgics*, whose farmers operate under a cycle motivated by *labor* (*redit agricolis labor actus in orbem* [*Georg.* 2.401]).[43] That implicit *Romanitas* is appropriated to describe the green itself which is, as it were, girt (*cincta* [7]) with armor in preparation for a battle of sorts. That armor constitutes in effect the protection of the turf itself, which functions as a "green toga"[44] clothing a landscape (*et viridi donata toga de cespite puro* [8])[45] that is now preparing itself for a sport (*ludus* [9]) or

---

ceremony. Cf. Virgil, *Aen.* 6. 258-259; Horace, *Odes* 3.1. William Somervile's "The Bowling Green" satirically categorizes such upper-class competitors as attorneys (17); parsons (18); whigs, papists, and high-flyers (19); aldermen and squires (20); quacks and writers (21).

[42] For the line-ending, cf. Virgil, *Georg.* 4.340: *altera tum primos Lucinae experta labores*. All quotations are from *Virgil: Georgics*, ed. R.F. Thomas (Cambridge, 1988), 2 vols.

[43] Contrast Samuel Bentley, "The Bowling Green," *Poems on Various Occasions*, 134, lines 2-4: "For there the softest mossy grass is found,/Where browse the sheep, and the sweet-breathing cow,/Untouch'd, uninjur'd by the galling plow."

[44] Cf. Dillingham's appropriation of the toga metaphor on a linguistic level to describe Theodore Bathurst's Latin verse rendering of Spenser's *The Shepheardes Calendar*. See 10 above.

[45] Cf. Antoine-Joseph Dezallier d'Argenville, *The Theory and Practice of Gardening* (London, 1728), 77: "A Bowling-Green is one of the most agreeable Compartments of a Garden, and, when 'tis rightly placed, nothing is more pleasant to the Eye. Its hollow Figure cover'd with a beautiful Carpet of Turf very smooth, and of a lively green."

perhaps the eventual splendors of a triumphal celebration (*magnis celebranda triumphis* [9]). But is not this a rather incongruous marriage between the rural and the civic, between the world of nature and that of human industry? The flattening of the land is depicted in terms suggestive of the gradual civilization of humankind and the recourse to pseudoindustrial activities evocative of an iron as opposed to a golden age. The natural landscape has been reworked, refined, and remolded to accommodate man-made constructions. Thus the waters of Avon are "compelled to bear the yoke" that is Wansford's bridge (*cogitur unda/ferre iugum* [1-2]) as though the river itself constituted a beast of burden now shouldering an anti-pastoral, anti-georgic weight. And the site is somewhat artificially hedged off (*postquam cincta est vivae munimine sepis* [7])[46] and flattened by a stone roller (*volubile saxum* [12])[47] to prevent any tufts of grass from impeding the course of the bowls themselves (12-13).[48] The lines may have suggested Addison's equivalent though much more pejorative description of the relentless sickle (*improba falx* [5])[49] and the lawn roller (*saxum versatile* [*Sphaeristerium* 7]) that ruthlessly level the surrounding quasi-pastoral

---

[46] Cf. Samuel Bentley, "The Bowling-Green," *Poems on Various Occasions*, 135, lines 6-12: "Lo! Round the green, the flow'ry shrubs arise:/See flaunting wood-bines pendulous in air./Beneath the laurel see the lily fair,/The purple vi'let and the blushing rose,/And all the graces Flora can disclose;/Far-stretch'd the walks extend amid' the flow'rs/Thro' clumps, thro' groves, and ever-verdant bow'rs." For Dillingham's elaborate description of a hedge (and its associated topiary), cf. *Sepes Hortensis* discussed in chapter 4 below.

[47] Cf. Samuel Bentley, "The Bowling-Green," *Poems on Various Occasions*, 138, lines 15-20: "The buskin'd horse must with fit tackle bound,/Drag the huge roller turning slowly round;/This way and that way rolling shall the stone,/Make all the green its heavy pressure own,/Hard make the turf, and spread each mossy blade/ Effacing ev'ry stroke the scythe has made."

[48] Cf. Robert Howlett, *The School of Recreation* (London, 1696), 95: "Have your Judgment about you to observe and distinguish the Risings, Fallings and Advantages of the Places where you Bowl;" William Somervile, "The Bowling Green," 11-12: "With curious Eye then the press'd Turf he views,/And ev'ry rising Prominence subdues;" Samuel Bentley, "The Bowling Green," *Poems on Various Occasions*, 138, lines 11-14: "The broom the mossy crop must clear away,/And the long withy o'er the surface play,/Quick to and fro, reverberating pass,/And lash away each straggling blade of grass."

[49] Cf. Anon., *Sphaeristerium* 17: *pinguia tondendo castigat gramina messor*; Samuel Bentley, "The Bowling Green," *Poems on Various Occasions*, 138, line 9: "Now must the scythe be frequently employ'd."

landscape to form a bowling green,[50] a description reworked by William Somervile to convey in anti-pastoral terms the tyrannical trimming and mowing of the bowling-surface:

> A cruel tyrant reigns: Like Time, the Swain
> Whets his unrighteous Scythe; and shaves the Plain.
> Beneath each Stroke the peeping Flow'rs decay,
> And all th' unripen'd Crop is swept away.
> The heavy Roller next he tugs along,
> Whifs his short Pipe, or reals a rural Song.[51]

Later in Dillingham's poem the contrast between pastoral innocence and civilization, as it were, is highlighted in the personified landscape (itself clad in a green toga [8]) marveling at its new occupants clad in yellow (10).[52] For these *novi ... coloni* (10) now seem to displace the *agricola* (6) of old. The theme resurfaces toward the end of the poem in the groaning of the mountains and the terror experienced by a Nymph upon hearing the noise of applause (94-96).[53]

Such applause is only one part of the essential realism that lies at the heart of *Suleianum*, and it is to this that we now turn. The poem emphasizes that bowling games generally occur on prescribed days

---

[50] Addison, *Sphaeristerium* 5-8: *improba falx noctis parva incrementa prioris/desecat, exiguam radens a caespite messem;/tum motu assiduo saxum versatile terram/deprimit exstantem et surgentes atterit herbas*. On the anti-pastoral and Virgilian dimension of these lines, see Haan, *Vergilius Redivivus: Studies in Joseph Addison's Latin Poetry*, 91-92. Cf. Anon., *Sphaeromachia* 2-3: *planities quam .../laevigat aequali quacunque ex parte Cylindro*; Anon., *Sphaeristerium* 21-22: *et subigit crassus tubercula quaeque cylindrus/nec salebra in torso surgat iniqua solo*. Cf. Arthur Bedford's description of the flattening of the handball alley in *Lusus Pilae Palmariae* 3-4: *et versatile saxum/surgentem in nodos, planum depressit in aequor*.

[51] William Somervile, "The Bowling Green," 5-10.

[52] *miraturque novos aurata veste colonos* (10). This is in all likelihood a reference to the color of the sporting outfit worn by the bowling team. Cf. Samuel Bentley, "The Bowling-Green," *Poems on Various Occasions*, 139, lines 9-10: "Then groups of bowlers thronging shall be seen,/And glowing figures animate the Green." Dillingham strikes an ironic parallel between the bowlers clad in golden garb and the landscape endowed with a green "toga" of smooth turf (*et viridi donata toga de cespite puro* [8]).

[53] *totusque remugit/mons circum; trepidat mediis exterrita silvis/Nympha loquax, dubitans tanti quae causa triumphi* (94-96). By the end of the poem, however, Nymphs joyfully salute the winner. See lines 98-100.

(*dictis plerumque diebus* [15]),[54] and proceeds to outline specific details of the match itself. Thus the competitors are divided into two teams (*in partes itur* [16])[55] in a mock-heroic battle of sorts. For the opposing sides are described in allegorical terms as the rival Florentine aristocratic[56] factions Guelphs and Ghibellines, but with their fury now appeased[57] even if their political sparring is perhaps mirrored on a microcosmic level. Dillingham conveys the fact that bowling is a betting sport, warning: *nimio si pignore certes,/corrumpis ludum ne sit sincera voluptas* (20-21).[58] And other such elements of realism occur: in highlighting, for example, the respective weights of individual bowls:[59] a

---

[54] This is expanded by the anonymous translator of Dillingham's poem in Bodl. MS Eng. Misc.d.1., ff 45-47, at f. 45, lines 19-21: "Hither the Gentry, when they would with play,/Unbend theire cares, on a sun-shiny day,/Twice in a week resort."

[55] Cf. Anon., *Sphaeromachia* 9-12: *sacculus antiquam referens producitur Urnam,/ indice designans sumpto certamina Talo,/in binas acies; veros disiungit Amicos/partibus oppositis*; John Marchant, "The Bowling Green," 9-12: "But trifle no Time in Debate;/We Six must be Three against Three;/So hussle the Lots in a Hat,/And see who the Partners shall be;" William Somervile, "The Bowling Green," 24: "dispos'd in Pairs;" Anon., *Pila Pedalis* 7: *in partes seceditur*.

[56] The inclusion of a simile pertaining to the aristocracy is appropriate in view of the fact that the competitors in the bowling match itself constitute a *generosa cohors* (14).

[57] *in partes itur; tu Guelfus esto,/hic Gibelinus erit, furiis tamen ante remotis* (*Suleianum* 16-17). Cf. Deborah Parker's allegorical reading of the tenth canto of Dante's *Inferno* as a dramatized reconstruction of the political debate between Guelphs and Ghibellines (*Lectura Dantis: Inferno X*, in *Lectura Dantis* 1. no. 1 [Fall, 1987], 37-47). Addison alludes to a division among the bowling teams that may occur either intentionally or accidentally (*in partes turbam distinxerat aequas/consilium aut pars* [*Sphaeristerium* 18-19]). Cf. William Somervile, "The Bowling Green" 35: "The Champions, or Consent, or Chance divide." The element of "chance" involved may allude to the practice of drawing lots to determine the composition of the teams. Cf. Anon., *Sphaeromachia* 9-12 cited in note 55 above.

[58] Cf. Anon., *Sphaeromachia* 5-6: *quos aemulus ardor/impulit ad pugnas, aurique insana cupido*; Richard Seymour, *The Compleat Gamester*, 323-324: "The best Sport in it, is the Gamesters, and he enjoys it most who looks on and bets nothing. ... Have a Care you are not in the first Place rooked out of your Money;" Samuel Bentley, "The Bowling Green," *Poems on Various Occasions*, 141, lines 7-8: "Agree what premium shall reward the game,/Less for the prize ambitious than for fame;" 141, lines 13-16: "Ah! Let no great pecuniary prize,/Depress the bowler's breast, nor damp his joys;/Let not fell gaming with delusive face,/The noble bowling exercise disgrace." Bentley follows this with a diatribe against "Gaming, thou fiend!"

[59] Cf. Robert Howlett, *The School of Recreation* (London, 1696), 95: "The first and greatest Cunning to be observed in Bowling, is the right chusing your Bowl, which must be suitable to the Grounds you design to run on."

bowl with a heavier amount of metal can roll in a curve (25-26),[60] whereas a lighter bowl can proceed in a straight line (46-47).[61] We hear of the role of the clubhouse (*domus* [27]) as a source of shade and refreshment for the weary competitors and also as a store room for the bowls themselves (27-29).[62] Emphasis is placed on the key role played by the jack (*meta*),[63] which now metaphorically assumes the role of the

---

[60] *lateri immisum quas fusile plumbum/et docuit solidare gradus et ducere gyros* (*Suleianum* 25-26). Cf. Addison, *Sphaeristerium* 14-15: *quae infuso multum inclinata metallo/vertitur in gyros et iniquo tramite currit*; Masters, *Mensa Lubrica* 27: *seu plumbi ignavi massa est seu divitis auri*; Anon., *Sphaeristerium* 39: *adduntur lateri plumbi libramina fusi*; William Somervile, "The Bowling Green," 28: "Here weighty Lead infus'd directs their Course;" Samuel Bentley, "The Bowling Green," *Poems on Various Occasions*, 140, lines 11-12: "One side is light, and one is heavy found,/Giving the bias as it circles round."

[61] *minimi quae conscia plumbi/radit iter laevum interior* (*Suleianum* 46-47). Cf. Addison, *Sphaeristerium* 16-17: *quam parcius urget/plumbea vis motuque sinit procedere recto*.

[62] *stat iuxta domus exilis, gratissima fessis/umbra viris; eadem ludentibus arma ministrat,/hinc puer expromit sphaeras, hic nocte recondit* (*Suleianum* 27-29). Addison describes perspiring bowlers in search of breeze and shade (*lenia iam zephyri spirantes frigora et umbrae/captantur, vultuque fluens abstergitur umor* [*Sphaeristerium* 65-66]). Cf. Samuel Bentley, "The Bowling-Green," *Poems on Various Occasions*, 136, lines 12-18: "Behold the graceful attic story rise!/With easy turnings flights of steps are seen,/And the neat structure decorates the green:/Thither the pleas'd spectators may repair,/Below sit warm, above enjoy the air;/Here, too, the bowlers may their spirits chear,/Whene'er fatigue, or languor shall appear."

[63] *protinus emittit nullo molimine sphaeram/exiguam* (*Suleianum* 35-36). Cf. *seu circumducto metam contingere gyro* (32); *stringere metam* (44); *metaeque amplexibus haeret* (48); *abducit metam* (93). Cf. Masters, *Mensa Lubrica*, 42: *summa gaudet consistere meta*; Anon., *Sphaeromachia* 15-16: *facili conamine metam/currentem primus per Sphaeristeria mittit*. In Addison, the jack, an *orbiculus* (20), flies forth to assume this function (*evolat orbiculus, quae cursum meta futurum/designat* [20-21]). Cf. *stipantque frequentia metam* (*Sphaeristerium*, 27); *metae inclinata recumbit* (*Sphaeristerium*, 47). Addison's juxtaposition of *meta* and *futurum*, which does not occur in Virgil, may have been suggested by Dillingham's phrase *cursus haec meta futuri* (*Suleianum* 36). On the key role of the jack, cf. John Marchant, "The Bowling Green," 13-16: "The Jack I will throw,/And trace it along with my Bowl:/Hah! Rub-rub a thousand!-Where now!/How wide from the Jack does it roll?"; Samuel Bentley, "The Bowling-Green," *Poems on Various Occasions*, 140, lines 18-20 – 141, line 1: "And there the jack, diminutive in size:/'Tis at the jack the bowlers all must play,/And 'tis the jack directs the ready way/For each succeeding bowl." *Meta* is used of the football goal-post at Anon., *Pila Pedalis* 34.

turning post in a Virgilian chariot or ship race.[64] At the same time it is strikingly eroticized, as in a cleverly gendered inversion of proper names the traditionally termed "Jack" becomes "Helen" (*haec Helena est* [36]) courted by the bowls.[65] Then in a wistful makarismos: "happy is the one ... who rests at last in her arms" (37-38).[66] The erotic terms in which the jack is presented find an interesting parallel in the anonymous *Sphaeristerium*, which goes one stage further by eroticizing the entire game of bowls, presenting it as the courting of Penelope by her multitude of suitors.[67] In Dillingham, however, this jack, this "Helen" becomes in effect a Nymph venerated by a virtually prostrate bowler (*prono veneratur corpore Nympham* [40]).[68]

But to obtain the object of such veneration the bowler must show versatility. Indeed the poem depicts the sheer variety of shots cast: the bowl that approaches stealthily, insinuating its way alongside the jack

---

[64] In *Aeneid* 5, prior to the ship race, Aeneas had established an oak marker as the meta: *his viridem Aeneas frondenti ex ilice metam/constituit signum nautis pater* (*Aen.* 5. 129-130). All quotations are from *The Aeneid of Virgil*, ed. R.D. Williams (New York, 1982), 2 vols. Cf. Homer, *Iliad* 23.327-330, in which the turning post is none other than a tree stump: "There stands, about a fathom's height above the ground, a dry stump, of oak or pine, which rots not in the rain, and two white stones on either side of it are firmly set against it at the turning of the course." Translation is that of A.T. Murray, *Homer: Iliad*, rev. W.F. Wyatt (Harvard: Loeb Classical Library, 1999), II, 517. At 23. 334-336 Nestor tells Antilochus: "Pressing hard on it drive your chariot and horses close, and yourself lean in your well-plaited chariot a little to the left of your pair" (*ibid.*, 517). Cf. 23.338-340: "But let the near horse draw close to the post so that the hub of the well-made wheel seems to graze the surface" (*ibid.*, 519).

[65] Cf. *metaeque amplexibus haeret* (48).

[66] *felix qui limine primo/egressus tandem illius requiescit in ulnis* (37-38).

[67] "*haec Ithaci Coniunx esto*" (*sphaeramque minorem/proiicit*) "*haec vestris meta petenda globis*" (25-26). The poem as a whole, and in particular the role played by the jack (Penelope) and the competing bowls (her suitors) seems to invert and develop Penelope's proclamation at *Odyssey* 21. 75-77: "Whichever man among you proves the handiest at stringing the bow and shoots an arrow through every one of these twelve axes, with that man I will go" (Homer, *The Odyssey*, trans. E.V. Rieu [Penguin, 1966], 317-318).

[68] Cf. Anon., *Sphaeristerium* 63-64: *hic Dominae ante pedes conatu lassus anhelo/procumbit, speciem sed venerantis habet*. In *Lusus Pilae Palmariae* 21-24 Arthur Bedford compares the hand-ball's erratic bouncing to Dido's frenzied madness: *nunc sublime petit, nunc densa per ora virorum/transvolat; hinc retro, hinc obliquo tramite fertur./sic Dido infelix furiis agitata per urbem/se rotat, et nulla fruitur miseranda quiete.*

(48),[69] the bowl that runs too quickly (56),[70] as opposed to the sluggish shot whose movement is closely followed by its thrower and whose delay is vehemently rebuked (57);[71] the bowl cast in error (70 and 75).[72] It also describes the physical contortions of the bowler (*corpore torto* [58])[73] as he follows the bowl he has just cast in an attempt to influence its movement,[74] an attempt satirized by Dillingham in the Virgilian phrase

---

[69] *metaeque amplexibus haeret* (*Suleianum* 48). Cf. Addison, *Sphaeristerium* 28-29: *iam cautius exit/et leviter sese insinuat revolubile lignum*. Addison's *insinuat* finds a parallel in Masters, *Mensa Lubrica* 50: *spatio summo sese insinuavit*. Cf. Samuel Bentley, "The Bowling-Green," 158, lines 1-2: "Insinuates itself without one shock,/ Now slow it creeps—yet creeps—to reach the block."

[70] *nunc festinantem vocis moderatur habena* (*Suleianum* 56). Cf. Anon., *Sphaeromachia* 25-26: *insequitur currentem, atque anxius imminet orbi,/ obiurgatque fugas, et dat convitia ligno*. This is followed (at 28-32) by a simile of Apollo's pursuit of Daphne.

[71] *ignavum et sine honore globum nunc increpat* (*Suleianum* 57). Cf. Anon., *Sphaeristerium* 47-48: "*siste modo, modo curre, precor; pete sphaera sinistram,/ mox dextram,*" *clamat;* "*mox bene coepta bene;*" John Marchant, "The Bowling Green," 21-24: "Jack Bonny succeeds in his Throw,/And takes a more middling Course;/Is short by his creeping too slow,/Tho' he bawls at his bowl till he's hoarse;" Samuel Bentley, "The Bowling-Green," *Poems on Various Occasions*, 144, lines 3-5: "The bowl now languid, seeming near a stand,/The bowler waves it forward with his hand;" 154, lines 13-16: "The swain pursues it, and in angry mood,/Upbraids, and chides, the unattentive wood;/With pantomime gestures Flee! He cries;/But short, its race soon terminating, dies."

[72] *quid reliquos memorem, varius quos abstulit error?* (*Suleianum* 70). Cf. Virgil, *Ecl.* 8.41: *ut me malus abstulit error!* Cf. *devius errat* (*Suleianum* 75). The theme recurs at Addison, *Sphaeristerium* 40-41: *falsos/increpat errores*. Cf. Samuel Bentley, "The Bowling-Green," *Poems on Various Occasions*, 149, lines 7-8: "Devious it wanders, and still goes astray,/Wider and wider, from its destin'd way."

[73] Cf. Addison, *Sphaeristerium* 40: *distorto corpore*; Francis Quarles, "See how their curved Bodies wreath, and skrue/Such Antick shapes as Proteus never knew," cited in Robert Howlett, *The School of Recreation*, 96; Charles Cotton, *The Compleat Gamester*, 223: "Never did *Mimick* scrue his Body into all the Forms these Men do theirs; and it is an Article of their Creed, that the bending back of the Body, or scruing in of their Shoulders, is sufficient to hinder the Over-speed of the Bowl, and that the running after it adds to its Speed;" Samuel Bentley, "The Bowling-Green," *Poems on Various Occasions*, 145, lines 1-4: "This twists, and wreaths, in attitude of pain,/While his bowl travels o'er the level plain;/And like the sun-flow'r turning tow'rds the sun,/Turns, as he wishes that his bowl may run."

[74] Cf. William Somervile, "The Bowling Green," 90-92: "Quick after it he skuds, urges behind/Step after step, and now, with anxious Mind/Hangs o'er the Bowl, slow-creeping on the Plain,/And chides its faint Efforts, and bawls amain;" Samuel

quid non sibi somnia fingunt? (60).[75] Then there is the bowler who falters, totters (72-75) and becomes an object of ridicule and laughter (*tota ridendus arena* [76]).[76] As such he takes his place alongside Homer's Ajax laughed at by the spectators of the foot race as he is covered in the slime in which he has slipped (*Iliad* 23.784) or Virgil's Menoetes who (in the ship race) is likewise ridiculed as he is flung overboard by Gyas (*Aeneid* 5. 181-182).[77]

In fact the poem as a whole frequently interacts with aspects of the anniversary games for Anchises described in *Aeneid* 5 (in a striking

---

Bentley, "The Bowling-Green," *Poems on Various Occasions*, 145, lines 5-6: "This, not contented with a distant view,/His running bowls will step by step pursue." Cf. Dugald Stewart, *Elements of the Philosophy of the Human Mind* (London, 1792-1827), III, 172-173: "A person, for example, who plays at bowls, and who is deeply interested in the game, while he follows the bowl with the eye, naturally accompanies its deflections from the rectilinear course, with correspondent motions of his body; although it cannot well be imagined, that, in doing so, he conceives himself to be projected from his own hand, and rolling along the ground like the object about which his thoughts are so strongly engrossed. Such, however, is his anxious solicitude about the event, that he cannot restrain his body from following in its [the bowl's] movements, the direction of his wishes; nor can he help fancying, while the event is yet in suspense, that it is in his power to forward it by a verbal expression of his wish, or even by a mental expression of his will." Interestingly Stewart cites Addison, *Sphaeristerium* 26-43, in support of his argument.

[75] The phrase echoes Virgil, *Ecl.* 8.108 (of deluded lovers) *an, qui amant, ipsi sibi somnia fingunt?* For satirical criticism of this attempt by the bowlers to influence the movement of the bowls, cf. Charles Cotton, *The Compleat Gamester*, 224: "How senseless these Men appear, when they are speaking Sense to their Bowls, putting Confidence in their Intreaties for a good Cast!" Cf. William Somervile, "The Bowling Green," 106-107: "Alas! How frail is ev'ry mortal Scheme!/We build on Sand, our Happiness a Dream." Cf. Dugald Stewart, *Elements of the Philosophy of the Human Mind*, III, 173: "Hence it is, that when the bowl takes a wrong bias, he is apt to address it, as if it could listen to, or obey his voice;—his body, in the mean time, *not*, as before, accompanying the motion of the bowl, but eagerly bending to the opposite side of the mark."

[76] Cf. Addison, *Sphaeristerium* 36-37: *nec risus tacuere globus cum volvitur actus/infami iactu*; Masters, *Mensa Lubrica* 29-30: *dextram comitatur inertem/et pudor, et risus, cassique infamia iactus*. Cf. Samuel Bentley, "The Bowling-Green," *Poems on Various Occasions*, 150, lines 9-12: "He sees his error with a wild surprise,/Midst hissing, clapping, universal noise;/Friends, foes, spectators, then at once combine,/And in a peal of taunting laughter join."

[77] On this episode, cf. Addison, *Spectator* 279 (19 January 1712: ed. Bond, II, 589): "I remember but one laugh in the whole *Aeneid*, which rises in the fifth book upon Menoetes, where he is represented as thrown overboard and drying himself upon a rock."

reinvention of the funeral games for Patroclus in *Iliad* 23) as a single bowling match seems to incorporate features from a whole variety of those Virgilian sports, but primarily from the foot race and the ship race. At times the behavior of several of Virgil's sports participants is mirrored or conflated in an individual bowler's action or reaction.

Even before the game proper a Virgilian intertext is signaled. As the rival bowling teams are established, the terms and conditions of the match are expounded (16-26) and epitomized in the following proclamation: *sed neque pro nuda iubeo te laude pacisci* (19). The statement recalls and inverts the quasi-heroic gravity afforded the participants in Virgil's ship race, in which the leaders strive to retain the glory of their positional advantage (*vitamque volunt pro laude pacisci* (*Aen.* 5. 230). But in this bowling game neither greed (*avaritia* [18]) nor glory (*laus* [19]) are to act as the motivating force.[78] Instead two types of prizes are recommended: one for the victor and a consolation prize for the loser, a custom which in itself is described as one pertaining to the ancients (*veterum ritus* [22]).[79] Both this and more generally the role of herald in Dillingham's poem recall the introductory announcements and subsequent actions of Aeneas.[80] Before the foot race, for example, Aeneas promises gifts (*munera* [5.247]) for all the runners (*nemo ex hoc numero mihi non donatus abibit* [*Aen.* 5.305]),[81] while after the race he not only announces the prizes to be awarded to first, second and third place, but also presents a consolation prize to Salius[82] and a special prize to Nisus.[83] Likewise in announcing the boxing competition (*Aen.*

---

[78] Cf. Samuel Bentley, "The Bowling Green," *Poems on Various Occasions*, 141, lines 7-8: "Agree what premium shall reward the game,/Less for the prize ambitious than for fame."

[79] *laudo tamen veterum ritus qui munera bina/praemia victori statuunt solatia victo* (*Suleianum* 22-23). Cf. Samuel Bentley, "The Bowling Green," *Poems on Various Occasions*, 131, lines 7-8: "And while each artist for the prize contends,/The victor, and the vanquished, still are friends."

[80] In the anonymous *Sphaeristerium* this role is assumed by a female, Penelope herself: *orbibus hic positis, "hoc" inquit femina "ludo/seria sunt vobis iam peragenda, proci./haec Ithaci Coniunx esto" (sphaeramque minorem/proiicit)* (23-26).

[81] Cf. Achilles at *Iliad* 23. 262-270.

[82] *immane leonis/dat Salio villis onerosum atque unguibus aureis* (*Aen.* 5.351-352).

[83] *clipeum efferri iussit* (*Aen.* 5.359).

5.362ff.), Aeneas offers a bullock for the victor and a sword and a helmet as a consolation prize for the vanquished.[84]

But Dillingham's description of the bowlers and at times the personified bowls themselves[85] seems to conflate a variety of Virgilian competitors. Thus as Sylvius takes the initiative (*primus ibi ante omnes in arenam Sylvius heros/descendit* [30-31]) he resembles both Gyas in the ship race (*effugit ante alios primisque elabitur undis* [Aen. 5.151]) and more strikingly Nisus, who takes the lead in the foot race and darts ahead in front of the others (*primus abit longeque ante omnia corpora Nisus/emicat* [Aen. 5.318-319]).[86] But where Gyas and Nisus fail, Sylvius will eventually succeed. And Dillingham actually names another of the competitors Nisus, the bowler par excellence, than whom no one is more outstanding whether in casting a bowl, in reaching the jack, in dislodging an opponent's throw, or in outrunning an opponent's shot (43-45).[87] His Nisus, however, recalls yet another Virgilian competitor. Nisus's bowl, because of its lesser amount of lead, can follow an inner left-hand path (*radit iter laevum meliorque priorem/detrudit spatio* [47-48]).[88] This personified bowl[89] recalls the behavior (in Virgil's ship race) of Cloanthus, who had likewise traced an inside path to the left (*radit iter laevum interior* [5. 170]), steering in-between the ship of Gyas and the

---

[84] *Sic ait, et geminum pugnae proponit honorem,/victori velatum auro vittisque iuvencum,/ensem atque insignem galeam solacia victo* (Aen. 5.365-367).

[85] On the personification of the bowls, cf. their equation with erotically resplendent dancers (*sphaeras splendore coruscas* [24]) taught how to dance in circles (*ducere gyros* [26]).

[86] Addison uses the verb *emicat* (*Sphaeristerium* 25) to describe a series of bowls suddenly cast one after the other.

[87] *excipit hunc Nisus, quo non praestantior alter,/sive globum versare manu seu stringere metam,/sive hostem turbare loco seu vincere cursu* (Suleianum 43-45). Line 43 may contain a proleptic irony since it recalls *Misenum Aeoliden, quo non praestantior alter* (Aen. 6. 164), who died when he challenged Triton to a trumpet contest. Compare Arthur Bedford's description of one of the competitors in a handball match at *Lusus Pilae Palmariae* 29-30: *hic forte astabat quo non praestantior alter/aut torquere pilam, propriae aut iactantior artis*.

[88] In Addison, a weakly cast bowl traces a path (*radit iter* [24]), tending toward a slight curve until, its original force gradually expended, it comes to rest: *at illa/ leniter effusa exiguum quod ducit in orbem/radit iter, donec sensim primo impete fesso/subsistat* (Sphaeristerium, 22-25).

[89] Cf. Pope's personification of playing cards in *Rape of the Lock* 3.44: "Draw forth to Combat on the Velvet Plain."

rocks themselves, and thereby overtaking him.[90] Whereas in Virgil, Cloanthus passed Gyas (who until then was in first position [*priorem* [170]) and left the *meta* behind (*metis ... relictis* [171]), Dillingham's bowl dislodges the leader (*priorem* [47]) from its space, and in pseudoerotic language clings to the *meta*.

Likewise wayward shots cast by faltering bowlers (*seu titubante pede et duplicato tramite vectus* [73]) seem to recall tottering and stumbling participants in their Virgilian counterpart: the athletic Nisus slipping in blood (*Aen.* 5.328-329)[91] or the stumbling boxer Entellus (*Aen.* 5.447-448).[92]

Such Virgilian intertexts, it might be argued, afford a level of grandeur to the game itself and as such contribute to the mock-heroic tone. This is also achieved by the Romanization of the whole. Dillingham's very brief reference to the *palaestra* (81) equates the bowlers with Roman wrestlers, whose custom it was to oil themselves before engaging in the *palaestra* (9). The theme is developed by Addison,[93] whose bowls run over a verdant *palaestra* (*Sphaeristerium* [9]) and are described as "anointed" and "glistening with oil" (*uncta, nitens oleo* [*Sphaeristerium* 10]). Indeed *Sphaeristerium* was a term employed in classical architecture to indicate a large space or room attached to the Roman baths (*thermae*). Here bathers would play ball games (usually prior to having a bath),[94] wash, and perhaps anoint

---

[90] *Aen.* 5. 169-171: *ille inter navemque Gyae scopulosque sonantis/radit iter laevum interior subitoque priorem/praeterit et metis tenet aequora tuta relictis.* The phrase recurs later in the ship race as Mnestheus is compared to a dove skimming its way in clear light without any movement of its swift wings: *mox aëre lapsa quieto/radit iter liquidum celeris neque commovet alas* (*Aen.* 5. 216-217).

[91] *levi cum sanguine Nisus/labitur infelix* (*Aen.* 5.328-329). Cf. Pope, *Dunciad* 2.69-74 where Curll slips and falls in a pool of excrement.

[92] *ipse gravis graviterque ad terram pondere vasto/concidit* (*Aen.* 5.447-448).

[93] See Haan, *Vergilius Redivivus: Studies in Joseph Addison's Latin Poetry*, 92-94.

[94] On ball games and Roman baths cf., for example, Pliny, *Epist.* 3.1.8: *ubi hora balinei nuntiata est (est autem hieme nona, aestate octava), in sole, si caret vento, ambulat nudus. deinde movetur pila vehementer et diu; nam hoc quoque exercitationis genere pugnat cum senectute. lotus accubat et paulisper cibum differt.* Text is that of *C. Plini Caecili Secundi Epistularum Libri Decem*, ed. R.A.B. Mynors (Oxford, 1963). Cf. Seneca, *Epist.* 56: *si vero pilicrepus supervenit et numerare coepit pilas, actum est.* Text is that of *L. Annaei Senecae Ad Lucilium Epistulae Morales*, ed. L.D. Reynolds (Oxford, 1965). On Augustus playing ball, cf. Suetonius, *Divus Augustus*, 83: *ad pilam primo folliculumque transiit.* Text is that of *Suetonius: Divus Augustus (De Vita Caesarum Liber II)*, ed. M.A. Levi (Florence, 1951).

themselves. Roman *thermae* possessed a *palaestra* of their own, a general peristylar sports area to which might be annexed the *sphaeristerium* itself.[95]

Ultimately, however, it is in the description of bowling as an epic battle and of the bowls themselves as warring heroes[96] that the mock-heroic comes to the fore. This is achieved by the implementation of a military metaphor throughout. Thus the bowls constitute "arms" (*arma* [28])[97] to be used against the "enemy."[98] The bowler must burst through (*perrumpere* [34]) the *hostiles ... turmas* (34),[99] and dislodge the enemy (*hostem turbare loco* [45]). Such an attempt is presented as the wish to remove an opponent from his position on a wall that is now captured (*ille volens capto Nisum detrudere muro* [61]),[100] but when unsuccessful the bowler can only waste his strength upon the empty breezes (*inque auras vires effundit inanes* [62]). The successful bowler is a hero (*Sylvius heros* [30]) possessed of ideal Roman qualities (*multa virtute insignis et arte* [31]),[101] and the winning shot is one which dissipates the enemy

---

[95] On the association of sports with Roman baths, see John Ward, *Roman Era in Britain* (London, 1911), 96: "Physical exercise was a concomitant of the bath. Even domestic baths sometimes had their tennis-court (*sphaeristerium*), as had Pliny's. In most of the public baths there was a spacious court (*palaestra*) with porticoes, exedrae, swimming-bath, etc., and other conveniences for outdoor recreation, ball-playing being a favourite pastime." See also Salvatore Aurigemma, *The Baths of Diocletian and the Museo Nazionale Romano*, trans. J. Guthrie (Fifth edition Rome: Istituto Poligrafico Dello Stato, 1963); Inge Nielsen, *Thermae Et Balnea* (Denmark, 1993).

[96] Cf. Pope, *Rape of the Lock* in which playing cards are given grandiose epic names: Spadillo [Ace of Spades] (3.49), Manillo [two of trumps] (3. 51), Basto [Ace of Clubs] (3.54), Pam [Jack of Clubs] (3.61), Amazon [Queen of Spades] (3.67).

[97] Cf. Addison, *Sphaeristerium* 19: *quisque suis accingitur armis*; Anon., *Sphaeristerium* 30: *arripit et cupida quilibet Arma manu*; Pope, *Rape of the Lock* 3.29: "Strait the three Bands prepare in Arms to join"; 3.47: "Now move to War her Sable Matadores"; 3.65: "both armies to Belinda yield."

[98] Cf. Addison, *Sphaeristerium* 48-49; Anon., *Sphaeristerium* 57.

[99] The phrase recurs in Arthur Bedford, *Lusus Pilae Palmariae* (68) (of rival competitors in a handball match).

[100] Cf. William Somervile, "The Bowling Green," 189-192: "So at some bloody Siege, the pond'rous Ball/Batters with ceaseless Rage the crumbling Wall,/(A Breach once made) soon galls the naked Town,/Riots in Blood, and heaps on heaps are thrown."

[101] Cf. *Aeneid* 5. 705 (of Nautes): *multaque insignem reddiderat arte*.

phalanxes, causing "death" all about (*ruptasque phalanges/dissipat hostiles, huc illuc funera spargens* [90-91]).[102]

The whole is highlighted by the occurrence of an epic simile (64-69) to convey the speed or efficiency of the participants.[103] Dillingham applies this to the defenders as opposed to the attackers. In language reminiscent of the behavior of Virgil's bees, bowls encircling the jack are likened to Roman youths in camp protecting their leader.[104] Here, as elsewhere in Dillingham, they do so in a clever fusion of the inanimate and the animate. And as Sylvius casts his winning shot, he becomes a second Jupiter of sorts, brandishing a weapon from a hand of thunder (*fulminea vibrata manu* [[90]]).[105] Nonetheless he is proclaimed by the

---

[102] Cf. William Somervile, "The Bowling Green," 183: "Bowls dash'd on Bowls confounded all the Plain;" 192: "And heaps on heaps are thrown;" Anon., *Pila Pedalis* 21-22: *corpora tum passim, nequicquam fortia, campo/sternuntur*; Pope, *Rape of the Lock* 3.80: "With Throngs promiscuous strew the level green."

[103] Both Virgil and Addison employ an epic simile (that of a chariot race). In *Aeneid* 5, as the signal is given for the commencement of the ship race, the rowers advance. Their movement is compared to that of chariots (*non tam praecipites biiugo certamine campum/corripuere ruuntque effusi carcere currus* [Aen. 5. 144-145]). Virgil continues: *nec sic immissis aurigae undantia lora/concussere iugis pronique in verbera pendent* (Aen. 5. 146-147). Cf. *Iliad* 23. 362-372, in which the charging horses quickly leave the ships behind. In Addison, as a rival tries to get the upper hand against his opponent, whose hit is resting alongside the jack, he stoutly casts his bowl: its power and speed are compared to a charioteer leaving the starting gate at Elis, and seeing buildings whizzing past: *haud ita prosiliens Eleo carcere pernix/auriga invehitur cum raptus ab axe citato/currentesque domos videt et fugientia tecta* (Sphaeristerium 52-54). Cf. Masters, *Mensa Lubrica* 8-10: *Romani credas spatium te cernere Circi/aut stadium Elei, lustro redeunte, Tonantis./utque Coloratas mirata est Roma Quadrigas*; *Mensa Lubrica* 38-42: *vere ille Argenteus orbis,/et dignus splendore suo qui Carcere pernix,/evolat et (cursum accedens tenui stridore)/lineolam post se linquit, neque limine Campi/contentus, summa gaudet consistere Meta.*

[104] Cf. *Georgics* 4.75-76: *et circa regem atque ipsa ad praetoria densae/miscentur magnisque vocant clamoribus hostem*. While Dillingham's simile is very different from those employed by Virgil and Addison, it is interesting to note that lines 67-68 (*tutaturque ducem, multoque satellite cingit./haud aliter Nisum socii fido agmine cingunt* ...) find a parallel in Addison, *Sphaeristerium* 55-56: *si tamen in duros, obstructa satellite multo,/impingat socios.* Cf. Samuel Bentley, "The Bowling Green," *Poems on Various Occasions*, 156, lines 11-12: "When round the jack the military beaux,/Lay cast on cast, and ev'ry passage close."

[105] Cf. Anon., *Sphaeromachia* 39-40: *orbatum toto mittit conamine Fulmen,/impingitque globos, confundens Orbibus Orbes*; 42-43: *vix diri fulmina Martis/obsessas quatiunt Urbes maiore tumultu.*

Nymphs (*"Sylvius" ingeminant: "ex illo tempore nobis/Sylvius; inque illis notissima nomina silvis"* [99-100]) in terms that integrate this quasi-divine victor into the pastoral landscape, which has formed the setting for that victory. Their salutation evokes the concluding lines of Virgil's seventh Eclogue as Meliboeus announces: *ex illo Corydon Corydon est tempore nobis* (*Ecl.* 7. 70). In his aims and aspirations, his manifold emotions, and his spirit of emulation perhaps a seventeenth-century bowler is not after all so very far removed from a Virgilian shepherd competitively producing his pastoral music.

Chapter 2

Ringing Classical Bells: *Campanae Undellenses*

Pastoral music lies at the very heart of Dillingham's *Campanae Undellenses*, which takes as its subject the peal and indeed the appeal of tolling bells. As such it is comparable perhaps with some vernacular verses prefixed to Thomas White's *Tintinnalogia or The Art of Ringing* (1671):

> What Musick is there that compar'd may be
> To well-tun'd Bells enchanting melody!
> Breaking with their sweet sound the willing Air,
> And in the list'ning ear the Soul ensnare;
> The ravisht Air such pleasure loth to lose,
> With thousand Echoes still prolongs each close;
> And gliding streams which in the Vallies trills,
> Assists its speed unto the neighbouring Hills.[1]

But the focus of Dillingham's poem is not so much on the actual bells themselves, but on the memories awakened in the listener, combined with an analysis of the accompanying emotional sensibilities. In this respect it seems somewhat ahead of its time, pre-empting as it does the treatment of the theme by eighteenth-century and Romantic poets. Such poets tend to emphasize both aural and emotional sensibilities, interrogating the effect of the tolling as it gradually wafts upon the breeze. And this operates on both a neo-Latin and a vernacular level. It is hardly a coincidence that in the mid-eighteenth century Dillingham's poem was anthologized by Vincent Bourne in his edition of the *Musae Anglicanae*,[2] for Bourne himself would compose two Latin poems on the subject, not without a backward glance at Dillingham's treatment.[3]

---

[1] "On the Ingenious Art of Ringing," prefixed to Thomas White, *Tintinnalogia or The Art of Ringing* (London, 1671), A3^r.

[2] *Musae Anglicanae Editio Quinta* (London, 1741), I, 244-248.

[3] See in general Haan, *Classical Romantic: Identity in the Latin Poetry of Vincent Bourne*, 100-103.

Bourne's *Certamen Musicum*, first published in 1734,[4] takes as its theme two different types of tolling produced by the bells of two Thames-side churches: St Mary-le-Bow and St Bride's (i.e., Wren's church on Fleet Street), which possess eight and twelve bells respectively. The tolling produced by the latter is light and swifter; that produced by the former is weighty and slower. Such a disparity is replicated both syntactically and rhythmically in a poem whose language mirrors the sounds themselves.[5] Likewise Bourne's short Latin epigram on the theme, entitled *Si Propius Stes, Te Capiet Minus*,[6] first published in 1743, shows how the harmony produced by the bells of St Mary Overie, London, is enhanced by the perspective of distance, thereby awakening enraptured awe in the listener. Or as George Orwell would later put it:

> All the while that they were talking the half-remembered rhyme kept running through Winston's head. Oranges and lemons, say the bells of St Clement's; You owe me three farthings say the bells of St Martin's! It was curious, but when you said it to yourself you had the illusion of actually hearing bells, the bells of lost London that still existed somewhere or other, disguised and forgotten. From one ghostly steeple after another he seemed to hear them pealing forth. Yet so far as he could remember he had never in real life heard church bells ringing.[7]

But if the tolling bell awakens memories, so too does it epitomize timelessness itself. Or as T.S. Eliot states:

---

[4] *Poematia, Latine Partim Reddita, Partim Scripta: a V. Bourne, Collegii Trinitatis Apud Cantabrigienses Aliquando Socio* (London, 1734), 140.

[5] See Haan, *Classical Romantic: Identity in the Latin Poetry of Vincent Bourne*, 100-101.

[6] Bourne's poem was first published in *Poematia, Latine Partim Reddita, Partim Scripta: a V. Bourne, Collegii Trinitatis Apud Cantabrigienses Aliquando Socio Tertio Edita Adiectis ad Calcem Quibusdam Novis* (London, 1743), 231. Its title inverts Horace's famous dictum (*Ars Poetica* 361-365) comparing reader response to poetry with the respective advantages afforded by closer and more distant perspectives of a painting. See Haan, *Classical Romantic: Identity in the Latin Poetry of Vincent Bourne*, 101-102.

[7] George Orwell, *Nineteen Eighty-Four*, ed. Bernard Crick (Oxford, 1984), 242. The St Clement's alluded to is either St Clement Danes or St Clement's Eastcheap, London. St Martin's is in all likelihood identifiable as St Martin-in-the Fields, London since 'five farthings' presumably refers to the moneylenders on St Martin's Lane.

> The tolling bell
> Measures time not our time, rung by the unhurried
> Ground swell, a time
> Older than the time of chronometers, older
> Than time counted by anxious worried women
> Lying awake, calculating the future,
> Trying to unweave, unwind, unravel
> And piece together the past and the future,
> Between midnight and dawn, when the past is all deception,
> The future futureless, before the morning watch
> When time stops and time is never ending;
> And the ground swell, that is and was from the beginning,
> Clangs
> The bell.[8]

Indeed the timelessness of Dillingham's poem becomes apparent upon closer inspection. For while the piece is strangely forward-looking, so too does it cast a backward glance to things classical, more specifically to the Latin poetic corpus of Virgil, with which it interacts on a variety of levels. At times such interaction locates the piece in a pastoral world, at others in settings more accurately describable as georgic or heroic, now wistfully recollected and recreated.

From the outset it is the quasi-pastoral that comes to the fore. The poem's opening lines are marked by their stillness and silence as outdoor activities and the accompanying din of the human voice have ceased. Such silence is mirrored in the natural world, conveyed by a series of negative statements: winds do not disturb the tranquil air (*nulli tranquillum turbabant aera venti* [3]) while the clouds do not dare to defile the clear sky (*nec coelum audebant nubes temerare serenum* [4]), the long vowel sounds recreating the stillness of the sound of silence that they celebrate. And the poem's *dramatis personae* are exiles who have lost a "pastoral" world in more than one sense. Having refused to subscribe to the Act of Uniformity, Dillingham had forfeited his posts as Master of Emmanuel College, Cambridge, and as Vice-Chancellor of the University with the result that he was thereby stripped of the religious and pastoral duties associated with those positions. Now he is *procul a Camo* (9), a "new inhabitant" of an "old countryside" (*veteris novus incola ruris* [9]), a lonely exile (*solus ego* [10]) even if he is in the company of a fellow exile Ferus (whose punning name is in fact a pseudonym for the ejected Presbyterian poet Robert Wild). In a sense they have in actuality

---

[8] T.S. Eliot, "The Dry Salvages," I, 35-48. Text is that of T.S. Eliot, *Four Quartets* (London, 1979).

realized a fate feared and experienced by such Virgilian shepherds[9] as Meliboeus in *Eclogue* 1[10] and Moeris in *Eclogue* 9.[11] In this instance, however, a lost pastoral paradise can perhaps be regained through the power of music and memory.

United in exile, they sit in front of a hearth, reciting their rustic muses (*solus ego en Ferus atque meus consedimus una/ante focum, agrestes recitantes ordine musas* [10-11]). And they do so in Virgilian terms: that *consedimus* reminiscent perhaps of such comments as those of Palaemon (*in molli consedimus herba* [*Ecl.* 3.55]) or Menalcas (*hic corylis mixtas inter consedimus ulmos?* [*Ecl.* 5.3]) or Meliboeus (*forte sub arguta consederat ilice Daphnis* [*Ecl.* 7.1]). In this instance, however, the pastoral landscape of grass, elms, or oaks has been replaced by the hearth itself (*ante focum*), a feature that is also nonetheless another part of the homely shepherd's world. Thus in *Ecl.* 5.70 Menalcas can imagine festivities *ante focum, si frigus erit*. Surprisingly, the traditional shepherd's flock is transmuted into a *grex stellarum* (5), thereby functioning on a cosmic level and feeding upon the whole of Olympus (*toto pascebat Olympo* [5]), a celestial pasture, so to speak. And the rustic muses (*agrestes ... musas* [11]) that constitute the subject of this particular song parallel the Virgilian speaker's contemplated song in *Ecl.* 6.8: *agrestem tenui meditabor harundine Musam*.

Into this pastoral setting that is both familiar and strange there intrudes a muse or music very different from that experienced by Virgilian shepherds. For this is produced not by the traditional shepherd's pipe or by the singing voice, but by the tolling of church bells. And far from being alien to this seventeenth-century pastoral locale, that *musica* (17) is depicted as though it were the lost or unattainable beloved about whom the shepherds of classical pastoral would frequently sing in

---

[9] On the theme of exile in Virgilian pastoral, see, among others, C.P. Segal, "*Tamen cantabitis, Arcades*: Exile and Arcadia in *Eclogues* 1 and 9," *Arion* 4 (1965), 237-266; B.F. Dick, "Vergil's Pastoral Poetic: A Reading of the First *Eclogue*," *American Journal of Philology* 91 (1970), 277-293; Christine Perkell, "On *Eclogue* 1. 79-83," *Transactions of the American Philological Association* 120 (1990), 171-181; Charles Martindale, "Green Politics: The *Eclogues*," in *The Cambridge Companion to Virgil*, ed. Charles Martindale (Cambridge, 1997), 107-124.

[10] *nos patriae finis et dulcia linquimus arva./nos patriam fugimus* (Virgil, *Ecl.* 1.3-4). Cf. *Ecl.* 1.64-66: *at nos hunc alii sitientis ibimus Afros,/pars Scythiam et rapidum cretae veniemus Oaxen/et penitus toto divisos orbe Britannos.*

[11] *O Lycida, vivi pervenimus, advena nostri/(quod numquam veriti sumus) ut possessor agelli/diceret: "haec mea sunt; veteres migrate coloni"* (Virgil, *Ecl.* 9. 2-4).

competitive rivalry. This is conveyed by Ferus through such terms of endearment as *dulcissima* (17), through the emotional verb *depereo* (18) used to describe his impassioned reaction to that music and, in an intensification of the quasi-amatory subtext, through close echoes of Virgil's love-sick Dido. Thus as the church-bells reawaken in Ferus memories of a distant past and of the religious duties that he once performed, he proclaims: *protinus agnovi veteris vestigia flammae* (19) in terms closely reminiscent of the widowed Dido's famous confession to her sister Anna of the fact that Aeneas has begun to resuscitate in her the traces of former passion (*agnosco veteris vestigia flammae* [*Aen*. 4. 23]).

If the poem's opening lines transport the reader to a Virgilian pastoral world, a world that is nonetheless subtly transformed and at times reinvented, the speaker's intervention seems to turn to a quasi-heroic and georgic setting. He too is inflamed by a similar love (*simili nonnullus tangor amore* [24]) of the music produced by the bells and of the memories that they enkindle in the human heart. He reflects on his childhood when he used to listen to the village bells of a rustic vicinity,[12] whose inhabitants would, when not engaged in ploughing, indulge in the pleasure of bell-ringing: *his, si quando labor curvi cessabat aratri,/ campanas pulsare sacras erat una voluptas* (29-30). At first sight the language is seemingly and perhaps surprisingly evocative of the disrespect for the plough that came to symbolize the loss of pastoral innocence in Latium as described in *Aeneid* 7.635-636: *huc omnis aratri/cessit amor*. In Dillingham, however, bell-ringing functions to enhance rather than to usurp a pastoral or georgic landscape while also constituting an alternative form of pleasure. But pleasure and pain frequently proceed hand in hand. For this music is hauntingly suggestive of loss. Thus as the speaker recalls how the bells rang out come day, come night (*sic veniente die, sic decedente canebant* [37]) he does so in language evocative of Orpheus's endless lamentation over the loss of Eurydice: *te veniente die, te decedente canebat* (*Georg*. 4. 466).[13] He

---

[12] Most likely a reference to the rustic surroundings of Northamptonshire where Dillingham spent his childhood. His father, Thomas Dillingham (d. 1647), was rector of Barnwell, All Saints, Northamptonshire. On the association of bells with memories of childhood, cf. F.S. Mahony, "The Shandon Bells," 1-8: "With deep affection,/And recollection,/I often think of/Those Shandon bells,/Whose sounds so wild would,/In the days of childhood,/Fling around my cradle/Their magic spells." Text is that of Leonard, ed. *A Book of Light Verse*, 355. On the parodic nature of the poem, see E.C. McAleer, "Understanding 'The Shandon Bells,'" *Modern Language Notes* 66.1 (1951), 474-475.

[13] For further evocations of Orpheus's lament cf. Dillingham's *Avicula* 35-36. See in general chapter 3.

longs to relive those childhood days when the tolling of bells lulled him to sleep or kept him awake (41-42).[14] In different ways then tolling bells and a lost Eurydice can epitomize a past that can never be recovered. For this speaker, however, in quasi-Romantic terms it is through the preserving power of memory that aspects of that lost past can at least begin to come to life again.

If the past can be regained through memory so too perhaps can a lost pastoral world. Just as *Eclogue* 1 afforded some sort of *consolatio* in Tityrus's description (to Meliboeus) of the rising Rome and a quasi-divine promise to ensure and safeguard the shepherd's domain, so in Oundle Dillingham has found some form of salvation. For he introduces the village and the *grandior ... cantus* (45) produced by its bells as surpassing all others[15] just as oak trees tower over hazel trees (*quae tantum villas inter caput extulit omnes/quantum inter corylos umbrosa cacumina quercus* [46-47]). The lines echo almost verbatim the description of the rising city of Rome as witnessed by Tityrus in *Ecl.* 1: *verum haec tantum alias inter caput extulit urbes/quantum lenta solent inter viburna cupressi* (*Ecl.* 1.24-25), a city in sharp contrast to the lowly and poverty-stricken world of pastoral simplicity: *pauperis et tuguri congestum caespite culmen* (*Ecl.* 1.68).

This description of Oundle is undoubtedly mock-heroic, but epic and pastoral can coexist in this seventeenth-century world. For now Virgilian poverty is proudly transformed into the thatched dwellings (*congesto cespite culmen* [49]) of a rustic vicinity that is impoverished yet simultaneously proud of its simplicity.[16] The village itself is strikingly

---

[14] *O illas dulces noctes cum ducere somnum/ad numeros licuit, vigilemque revisere vitam* (41-42). For a contrary viewpoint, cf. Giovanni Casa, *In Campanas*, 1-6: *o quae terrificos vicina e turre cietis/tot nocte aere sonos tinnulla, totque die,/si mihi venturae noctis dormire licebit/per tot tinnitus particulam misero:/nec cum defessos iam iam continget ocellos,/vos metuet subito diffugietque sopor.* Text is that of *Carmina Illustrium Poetarum Italorum*, ed. G.G. Bottari (Florence, 1689-1775), III, 281.

[15] Cf. F.S. Mahony, "The Shandon Bells," 25-32: "For memory, dwelling/On each proud swelling/Of the belfry knelling/Its bold notes free,/Made the bells of Shandon/Sound far more grand on/The pleasant waters/Of the River Lee."

[16] See, however, Dillingham's very real concern for the poverty of his deceased brother's vicarage at Oundle as conveyed in a letter to Sancroft dated 24 Nov. 1679 (Bodl. MS Tanner 147, f. 44): "There is a poor vicarage at Oundle in Northampton Shire of fifteen hundred communicants ... which is now vacant by the death of my Brother, who after greate paines taking in that curia dyed eight dayes since leaving a widdow and 6 small children but very meanly provided for. Which makes me the more sensible of the great want of maintenance for a curate in so considerable a place."

personified, depicted on the one hand as a virtual horseman riding upon the back of a mountain (51),[17] and on the other as a playful paddler, dipping its feet in the waters of the Avon (52).[18] And more than that: for if Oundle is a second Rome so too is this turreted village (*altaque turrigerum caput inter nubila condit* [54]) depicted in all its rustic regality as a second Dido (*ingrediturque solo et caput inter nubila condit* [*Aen.* 4.177]).[19]

And the city can aspire beyond the merely mortal. In a stunning personification the bells of the church are depicted as five Muses (*quinque sorores* [57]) possessed of varying sounds (*et queis vox pariter dispar* [58]), including both high and low,[20] with a combined and cumulative effect that causes Echo to tremble, and perhaps dislodges even the spirits of the dead from their abode (61-62). The salutary consequences of such music are highlighted: it can dispel care, purify the breezes, and even ward off evil spirits (63-64), who take flight in fear of the imminent prayerfulness signaled by the sound (66). Such Muses are multifaceted and toll on a variety of occasions (70-74).

The poem then zooms in on one festive occasion in particular, that of Restoration Day (29 May): *Caroli ... lux festa* (78),[21] while the associated imagery transports the whole to a quasi-divine plane. As soon as this festive day comes round the sisters hasten as Nymphs dance and sing songs (*pars pedibus plaudunt choreas, pars carmina dicunt* [105]) in

---

[17] *promissique sedens equitansque in tergore montis* (51).

[18] *Aufoniasque utrimque pedem demittit ad undas* (52). Cf. John Dyer, "Grongar Hill," 65-72: "Gaudy as the op'ning dawn,/Lies a long and level lawn/On which a dark hill, steep and high,/Holds and charms the wandering eye!/Deep are his feet in Towy's flood,/His sides are clothed with waving wood,/And ancient towers crown his brow,/That cast an aweful look below." Text is that of John Dyer, *Poems 1761* (Scolar Press, 1971).

[19] Cf. *Aeneid* 10. 767 (of Orion).

[20] Bourne's *Certamen Musicum* likewise differentiates between the various types of sound produced by bells of different weight: *Octo trans Tamisin campanis diva Maria,/cis Tamisin bis sex diva Brigetta sonat./haec tenues urget modulos properantius aedes,/alternat grandes lentius illa modos./nec quis in alterutro distinguat litore iudex/an magis haec aurem captet an illa magis./tantae est harmoniae contentio musica, turris/altera cum numeros, altera pondus habet.* Text is that of Haan, *Classical Romantic: Identity in the Latin Poetry of Vincent Bourne*, Appendix 1.

[21] Known as either Restoration Day or Oak-Apple Day, 29 May was appointed by Parliament as a Day of Thanksgiving. It was eventually dropped from the *Book of Common Prayer* in 1859.

a close echo of the celebrations in Virgil's Elysium (*pars pedibus plaudunt choreas et carmina dicunt* [*Aen.* 6. 644]). Among these Nymphs the most beautiful is Calliope (*quarum, quae forma pulcherrima, Caliopeia* [106]), who seems to parallel two female characters in *Aeneid* 1: the Nymph offered as a bribe by Juno to Aeolus (*quarum quae forma pulcherrima Deiopea* [*Aen.* 1.72]), and also perhaps Dido herself (*forma pulcherrima Dido* [*Aen.* 1.496]). And as they ring out they mirror a people's joy at the Restoration (*gaudentemque canit populum, Regemque reductum* [108]).[22] But this idyll is not without its own glimpses of realism, for combined with such festivities are the potent memories of the political dangers encountered by Charles (*pretiosa peric'la/tam cari capitis* [109-110]). The whole reaches a climax in an encomium of the restored king, and unqualified praise of his gentleness and righteousness. The lines are undoubtedly characterized by the hyperbole that typically underlies such royal flattery (after all, Dillingham had written in 1660 encomiastic Latin verses that were prefixed to a volume of Cambridge poems celebrating the Restoration),[23] but as the poem concludes, the focus shifts from the restoration of a king to that of a poet, whose exile in a pastoral retreat has at last given way to and even enhanced the power of song (*haec ego campanis super et super aere canoro* [129] ... *et cecini, et cecinisse iuvat* [134]). The lines mirror Virgil's poetic *sphragis*[24] to the *Georgics* (*Haec super arvorum cultu pecorumque canebam/et super arboribus, Caesar dum magnus ad altum/fulminat Euphraten, te ... cecini* [*Georg.* 4.559-566]). But if in Charles II Dillingham has found a second Augustus,[25] so too perhaps, like the ringing bells celebrated in the poem, has he found a music of his own. It is a music that seems to achieve a harmony between past and present, between classical and contemporary, between the public and the private worlds of the poem, evoking sensibilities that are perhaps most accurately described as quasi-

---

[22] Cf. *The Elegant Entertainer, and Merry Story-teller: Being a Valuable Collection of Diverting and Instructive Tales, Fables, and Other Curious Articles, Both in Prose and Verse* (London, 1676), 107: "Besides the common way of tolling bells there is also ringing, which is a kind of chimes used on various occasions in token of joy. This ringing prevails in no country so much as in England."

[23] See Appendix 3.

[24] On the *sphragis* ("seal," "signature"), see Thomas, ed. *Georgics*, II, 239.

[25] Cf. the possible equation of Charles and Augustus in the punning phrase: *augustos laeta celebrantem pace triumphos* (115). See also Appendix 3.

Romantic in their conception. Or as William Cowper[26] would later proclaim:

> There is in souls a sympathy with sounds;
> And, as the mind is pitch'd, the ear is pleas'd
> With melting airs, or martial, brisk, or grave:
> Some chord in unison with what we hear
> Is touch'd within us, and the heart replies.
> How soft the music of those village bells,
> Falling at intervals upon the ear
> In cadence sweet, now dying all away,
> Now pealing loud again, and louder still,
> Clear and sonorous, as the gale comes on. (*The Task* 6.1-10)[27]

---

[26] Cowper was himself a pupil of Vincent Bourne, and translated several of the latter's Latin poems into English verse. See Haan, *Classical Romantic: Identity in the Latin Poetry of Vincent Bourne*, 7-8, 102–103, 167-177.

[27] Text is that of *William Cowper: Poetical Works*, ed. H.S. Milford (Oxford, 1971). Cf. Cowper, "The Task," 1.174–175: "Tall spire, from which the sound of cheerful bells/Just undulates upon the listening ear"; Thomas Hood: "Dear Bells! how sweet the sound of village bells/When on the undulating air they swim!" ("Ode to Rae Wilson," 159-160.) Text is that of *The Complete Poetical Works of Thomas Hood*, ed. Walter Jerrold (London, 1906), 511.

Chapter 3

Two Classical Fables? From *Avicula* to Nemesis

Where *Suleianum* and *Campanae Undellenses* depict the variety of pleasures deriving from bowling and bell-ringing respectively, *Avicula* and *Nemesis a Tergo* turn to the world of nature and contemporary folklore to present in quasi-moralistic tones the danger and retribution attendant upon reckless ambition and theft. On the one hand they are typical of Dillingham's methodology in that here once again they seem to reinvent a classical world; on the other, they move beyond his practice to date. For these pieces can perhaps best be categorized as moralistic fables characterized by an implicit didacticism.

Avicula takes as its subject a young fledgling's attempt at flight after receiving instruction from her mother. It is a carefully wrought piece, of which Sancroft enthusiastically proclaimed: "if there be any fault in it, 'tis that it hath none at all, being, as some perhaps would say, over-labored already."[1] The poem, cast in Latin hexameters, describes the gradual stages of the fledgling's experience: her enticement by her mother from the nest, her associated trepidation, and her initial endeavor to fly. But when, following her mother's example, she gradually takes to the air, fear is displaced by reckless ambition and an over zealous soaring, which in turn leads to her misfortune in a headlong fall. Worthy of comparison and contrast perhaps is the treatment of the subject in James Thomson's vernacular poem "Spring" (1728):

> O'er the Boughs
> Dancing about, still at the giddy Verge
> Their Resolution fails; their Pinnions still,
> In loose Liberation stretch'd, to trust the Void
> Trembling refuse: till down before them fly
> The Parent-Guides, and chide, exhort, command,
> Or push them off. The surging Air receives

---

[1] Sancroft to Dillingham: 16 November 1677 (BL Sloane 1710, f. 214). Sancroft, however, proceeds to offer no fewer than nine suggestions for minor improvements to the piece. See, for example, notes 8, 15, 19, and 24.

> The plumy Burden; and their self-taught Wings
> Winnow the waving Element. On Ground
> Alighted, bolder up again they lead,
> Farther and farther on, the lengthening Flight;
> Till vanish'd every Fear, and every Power
> Rouz'd into Life and Action, light in Air
> Th'acquitted Parents see their soaring Race,
> And once rejoicing never know them more.
> ("Spring," 740-754)[2]

Like Dillingham, Thomson conveys the initial faltering of the fledging, its trepidation and reluctance to make trial of the air, its eventual audacity, emphasizing the central role played by the parental guide via a series of staccato verbs ("chide, exhort, command" [745]).[3] But there is an important difference. The fatally doomed precipitating *Avicula* has been displaced by a "soaring Race" (753), and a grieving mother has given way to parents who rejoice as they witness a successful flight.

Dillingham's poem, however, does not confine itself to a depiction of the fledgling's emotions and fate. Equally important is the representation of a mother bird's conflicting sensibilities and actions: her admixture of gentle advice, instruction, and rebuke; her teaching by example; her anxious expectation and anticipation as she sits perched upon a neighboring tree waiting for the fledgling to join her; then her tragic grief as she witnesses the fate of her chick, a grief conveyed in human terms as a mother beating her breast and proclaiming a funeral dirge for a lost daughter. Such anthropomorphism is in fact central to the poem's success. And it is both mirrored and achieved in terms of the Virgilian and Ovidian intertexts with which the piece engages.

On the one hand the poem is quasi-georgic in its conception. This seems to operate on two levels. Initially the birds mirror the behavior of Virgil's bees, but in the poem's closing moments they re-enact aspects of the Orpheus/Eurydice episode of *Georgics* 4. That the *avicula* and its mother should be cast in language reminiscent of Virgilian *apes* is perhaps hardly surprising, for in Virgil's didactic poem Dillingham would have found the locus classicus for the personification of the natural world and its creatures. Thus, just as the ideal site of the Virgilian hive is a location close to a tree which will afford "hospitable leaves" (*obviaque hospitiis teneat frondentibus* [*Georg.* 4.24]), so the birds' nest is positioned upon the branches of an hospitable elm (*hospitis ulmi* [3]). In

---

[2] Text is that of *Eighteenth-Century Poetry*, eds. David Fairer and Christine Gerrard (Oxford: Blackwell, 2004), 229.

[3] Cf. Dillingham, *Avicula* 8: *suadet, iubet, increpat, urget*.

both instances the dwelling or "nest"[4] is described in language reminiscent of the Roman household with its *lares* and *penates*. Thus Virgil's bees *fovere larem* (*Georg.* 4.43); *et patriam solae et certos novere penates* (*Georg.* 4.155) whilst in Dillingham the mother bird has hung[5] upon the tree a nest, which constitutes *patriam parvosque lares* [4]). In both the possible dangers of flight are signaled via the notion of entrusting oneself to the sky (*aut credunt coelo adventantibus Euris* [*Georg.* 4.192]/*credere coelo* [6]). But the miraculous vision of a swarm issuing from a hive and streaming through the sky (*Georg.* 4.58-61)[6] has now become the painful and pitiful sight of a failed flight that is strikingly individualized, beheld as it is by a lamenting mother who is also to some degree a second Orpheus.

In *Georgics* 4, Orpheus, upon losing his wife, Eurydice (after his fateful contravention of the divine decree by looking back at her as they were emerging from the underworld), articulates his sorrow in lugubrious tones. This is compared by Virgil in a famous simile (*Georg.* 4. 512-515) to the grief of a nightingale lamenting the death of her chicks, whom a ruthless ploughman has snatched while still fledglings from their nest.[7] The nightingale's *miserabile carmen* (*Georg.* 4.514) has become in Dillingham's version the mother bird's *lacrimabile carmen* (29), while the lamentation itself and its effect upon the surrounding landscape (*et maestis late loca questibus implet* [*Georg.* 4.515]) are now echoed in the depiction of the mother as *late loca questibus implens* (31).[8] For this is a poem in which creatures of the natural world both mirror and indeed transcend their human counterparts.

---

[4] Virgil uses *nidus* to describe the hive at *Georgics* 4.56: *progeniem nidosque fovent*.

[5] On a bird "hanging" her nest, cf. *Georgics* 4. 306-307: *ante/garrula quam tignis nidum suspenderat hirundo*.

[6] *hinc ubi iam emissum caveis ad sidera coeli/nare per aestatem liquidam suspexeris agmen/obscuramque trahi vento mirabere nubem,/contemplator* (*Georgics* 4.58-61).

[7] *qualis populea maerens philomela sub umbra/amissos queritur fetus, quos durus arator/observans nido implumis detraxit; at illa/flet noctem, ramoque sedens miserabile carmen/integrat, et maestis late loca questibus implet* (*Georgics* 4.511-515).

[8] This Virgilian phrase was suggested to Dillingham by Sancroft, who comments as follows upon an earlier version of the line: "The only thing I would add is that in the Lamentation of the old Lady-Bird for losse of her Daughter, at *mane, mane, improba, dixit* I would add a little mollifying *dixit* with the parenthesis (*Dicere vel visa est, late loca questibus implens*)" (Sancroft: Letter to Dillingham dated 16 November 1677. BL Sloane 1710, f. 214).

And this operates on the level of epic heroism. At times the language in which the birds are depicted is quasi-heroic. This occurs at key moments in the poem and not without proleptic irony. For example, as the mother teaches her chick how to fly, she assumes a quasi-pedagogical role in, as Sancroft terms it, "Nature's great Academie,"[9] soaring ahead, then returning to lead forth her fledgling. The erratic motion of coming and going (*itque reditque viam toties* [10]) is conveyed via a verbatim echo of Virgil's description in *Aeneid* 6.122 of the immortal Pollux's infernal journey (in place of his twin, Castor) for six months each year. Here, as elsewhere, the poem's intertextuality seems to signal that the flight itself is doomed, for the important difference in Dillingham's poem is that death *cannot* be ransomed. Though doomed, however, that flight is couched in epic language. When the overweening chick realizes that she is entrapped and that nothing but unknown paths of sky remain (*coelique profundi/ignotas restare vias* [41-42]) the quasi-heroic nature of her audacity is signaled via a verbal reminiscence of Evander's question to Aeneas about the purpose of his epic journey: *quae causa subegit/ignotas temptare vias* (*Aen.* 8.112-113). Similarly, when she perceives the danger in which she has placed herself by flying too high, the horror of that realization (*gravis ingruit horror* [42]) is conveyed in language evocative of Aeneas's professed acknowledgment of the grim reality of the Trojan war (*clarescunt sonitus armorumque ingruit horror* [*Aen.* 2.301]). And the military subtext is evoked in the mother's pseudo-Horatian question: *quo ruis?* (32),[10] a question likewise posed by Aeneas to his comrades overcome by martial frenzy and lust for blood (*quo ruitis? quaeve ista repens discordia surgit?* [*Aen.* 12.313]). Ultimately, however, the chick's flight is censured for its rash daring, a daring, which is in fact Icarian in essence.

The Icarian subtext of Dillingham's poem is facilitated by the fact that Ovid's accounts (in *Metamorphoses* 8 and *Ars Amatoria* 2) of the Daedalus/Icarus episode explicitly compare the mythological characters to birds. Thus in *Ars Amatoria* 2 the instruction provided by Daedalus to his son is compared to that of a mother bird to her chick (*erudit infirmas*

---

[9] Sancroft highlights the pedagogical dimension of the piece: "And now I am come to your Little Bird at Schole, learning to fly in Nature's great Academie." (Sancroft: Letter to Dillingham dated 16 November 1677. BL Sloane 1710, f. 214). Contrast Mrs. Lovechild, *A Miscellany in Prose and Verse for Young Persons* (London, 1795), 69: "The bird fluttering from its parent's nest needs no instruction to fulfil her task."

[10] Cf. Horace's grim querying of the horrors of civil war at *Epode* 7.1: *quo quo scelesti ruitis?* Text is that of *Horace: Epodes*, ed. David Mankin (Cambridge, 1995).

ut sua mater aves [*A.A.* 2. 66]).[11] Likewise in *Metamorphoses* 8 as Daedalus flies ahead of Icarus, his fear for his son's welfare is compared to that of a bird leading her young chick from the nest (*velut ales, ab alto/quae teneram prolem produxit in aëra nido* [*Met.* 8. 213-214]).[12] Throughout the *Avicula* mother bird and chick are represented in terms strikingly reminiscent of Daedalus and Icarus respectively. But the Ovidian bird similes and the contexts in which those similes occur function only as a point of departure for Dillingham's treatment.

In Ovid's versions Daedalus is depicted as instructing (*instruit* [*Met.* 8. 203])[13] and encouraging his son (*hortaturque sequi* [*Met.* 8. 215]), and as leading the way by his example (*me duce carpe viam* [*Met.* 8. 208]/*me pinnis sectare datis; ego praevius ibo:/sit tua cura sequi, me duce tutus eris* [*A.A.* 2.57-58]). The principles of the imminent flight are clearly articulated and enumerated: Daedalus warns his son to be careful not to fly too low in case he falls into the sea; likewise he must not fly too high in case the sun's heat melts the wax fastenings on his wings; instead he is to seek a middle path.[14] Like Daedalus, Dillingham's mother bird gently encourages her offspring (*hortatu hanc mulcet mater* [7])[15] while the Ovidian combination of instruction, admonition, and rebuke is now encapsulated not by recourse to direct speech but by an emphatic series of four staccato verbs as the mother persuades, commands, rebukes, and urges her chick (*suadet, iubet, increpat, urget* [8]). Like Daedalus (*ante volat* [*Met.* 8. 213]), she flies ahead (*ante volans* [19]), equally fearful for her offspring's fate (*comitique timet* [*Met.* 8. 213]; *multa timens* [22]), but

---

[11] Text is that of *Ovid: Amores, Medicamina, Faciei Femineae, Ars Amatoria, Remedia Amoris*, ed. E.J. Kenney (Oxford, 1994).

[12] Text is that of *Ovid: Metamorphoses*, ed. W.S. Anderson (Teubner, 1977). Cf. Valerius Flaccus, *Argonauticon* 7.375-377: *qualis adhuc teneros supremum callida fetus/mater ab excelso produxit in aera nido,/hortaturque sequi*. Text is that of *C. Valeri Flacci Argonauticon*, ed. Peter Langen (Hildesheim, 1964).

[13] Cf. *Met.* 8. 208-209: *praecepta volandi/tradit*.

[14] Ovid, *Met.* 8. 203-206: *instruit et natum "medio" que "ut limite curras,/Icare," ait "moneo, ne, si demissior ibis,/unda gravet pennas, si celsior, ignis adurat:/inter utrumque vola."* Cf. *Ars Amatoria* 2. 59-63: *"nam sive aetherias vicino sole per auras/ibimus, impatiens cera caloris erit;/sive humiles propiore freto iactabimus alas,/mobilis aequoreis pinna madescet aquis./inter utrumque vola."*

[15] Sancroft suggested this emendation to Dillingham's original phrase *hanc mater mulcet dictis*, stating: "*dictis* is pretty bold: why not *hortatu hanc mulcet mater*?" (Sancroft: Letter to Dillingham dated 16 November 1677 BL Sloane 1710, f. 214).

at the same time teaching by example and looking back out of concern for the well-being of her chick.[16]

Ovid's versions strike a homely contrast between the serious endeavors of Daedalus and the playful and ultimately reckless behavior of Icarus. Thus as his father is constructing the wings and carefully arranging the feathers in order, Icarus takes great pleasure in playfully snatching at those feathers that float along the breeze.[17] By contrast, the baby chick is consumed by fear from the outset, palpitating (*pectore toto/palpitat* [5-6]), fearing (*metuens* [6]), and possessing *timores* (7). It is a fear that will be rendered all too real. Just as Ovid's Icarus begins to rejoice in his daring flight (*cum puer audaci coepit gaudere volatu* [*Met.* 8. 223]/*cum puer incautis nimium temerarius annis* [*A.A.* 2.83]), a flight that is too lofty (*altius egit iter* [*Met.* 8. 225; *A.A.* 84]), so the chick is borne upon a flight that is excessively high (*ferri nimio in sublime volatu* [21])[18] while rejoicing in an ascent that is both celestial and, as Sancroft noted,[19] surprisingly cosmic (*iam caelum meditetur ovans, et cogitet astra* [25]).[20] In both instances such behavior is presented as the very antithesis

---

[16] *redux cessantem corripit* (9). Cf. *et nati respicit alas* (*Met.* 8. 216; *A.A.* 2.73).

[17] *quas vaga moverat aura,/captabat plumas* (*Met.* 8.197).

[18] Writing to Sancroft from Cambridge in June 1642, Dillingham uses the metaphor of birds perparing to fly to describe the restlessness of the university students at the end of term: *sed interim levant ales suas iuvenes ac si avolaturi* ... (Bodl. Tanner MS 63, f. 42). See 3-4 above.

[19] The phrase *et cogitet astra* was suggested by Sancroft, who remarked on an earlier version of this passage: "*Designare Astra* is a phrase that takes me not at all; I would say *et cogitet Astra*, to unite with *meditetur* just before. But what doth your day-bird (such I suppose her) to do with the starres? She goes to bed too soon to be acquainted with them. I would therefore say *atque aethera tranet*" (Sancroft: Letter to Dillingham dated 16 November 1677. BL Sloane 1710, f. 214). Cf. William Wordsworth, "To a Skylark," 1-2: "Ethereal minstrel! pilgrim of the sky!/Dost thou despise the earth where cares abound?" Text is that of *William Wordsworth: Poems*, ed. J.O. Hayden (Penguin, 1977); Shelley, "To a Skylark," 6-10: "Higher still and higher/From the earth thou springest/Like a cloud of fire;/The blue deep thou wingest,/And singing still dost soar, and soaring ever singest" Text is that of *The Poetical Works of Percy Bysse Shelley*, ed. Mary Wollstonecraft Shelley (London and New York, 1889).

[20] On the joys of an envisaged flight and the associated perception of the cosmos, cf. Francis Harding, *In Artem Volandi* 59-61: *tum me continuo ad Lunae felicia regna/proriperem velox, rediturus non nisi magno/argenti pariter libratus pondere et auri*. Text is that of *Musae Anglicanae* (London, 1741), 60; Thomas Gray, *Luna Habitabilis* 14-15: *o quis me pennis aethrae super ardua sistet/mirantem, propiusque dabit convexa tueri*. Text is that of Estelle Haan, *Thomas Gray's Latin Poetry: Some*

of filial piety. Thus Icarus *deseruitque patrem* (*A.A.* 2. 84)[21] only to be lamented by a *pater infelix* (*Met.* 8.231; *A.A.* 2.93), now no longer a father (*nec iam pater* [*Met.* 8.231; *A.A.* 2.93]). In Dillingham not even the chick's sense of *pietas* or regard for her mother (*cura parentis*) can change her fatally transgressive behavior.[22] All that remains is for the parent to call upon the offspring in vain. Thus the Daedalean twofold exclamation *"Icare ... /Icare, ... ubi es?"* (*Met.* 8. 231-232/*A.A.* 2.93-94) becomes the mother bird's plea that her offspring check her flight (*"dilecta, mane, mane, improba," dixit* [30]), a plea that is likewise twofold (*lugubri natam, natam bis voce vocabat* [35]). But all too late. For in *Ars Amatoria* 2 the father's words mirror a twofold exclamation proclaimed by the falling Icarus: *"pater, o pater, auferor!"* (91).[23] In the *Avicula* a mother's lament is reciprocated by a daughter's futile cry for help from a parent, a cry that can only go unheard (*saepe suam matrem non exaudita vocabat* [45]) as Dillingham's avian Icarus proclaims a lamentation of her own (*sed dum triste gemens luctus singultibus urget* [47])[24] and plunges to the ground.

Where *Avicula* conveys the moral of the danger of flying too high, Dillingham's *Nemesis A Tergo* emphasizes the inevitability of retribution for wrongdoing, citing a "proof" of the moral in question. Like the *Avicula*, this poem was sent by Dillingham to Sancroft. This is attested by the latter's reply in a letter dated 16 November 1677 in which he states: "I am much pleas'd with your Thief taken in the Marmor," and suggests the

---

Classical, Neo-Latin and Vernacular Contexts (Brussels: Collection Latomus 257, 2000), Appendix 1.

[21] Cf. *deseruitque ducem* (*Met.* 8.224).

[22] *non illam pietas, non illam cura parentis/abstrahere inde potest* (*Avicula* 26-27).

[23] Cf. Caelius Calcagninus, *Casus Icari*, 1-4: *Daedalus insuetis scindat licet aera pennis,/non cessat natum voce monere tamen:/"Icare, per medium tutissimus ibis."/Icarus exclamat "mi pater, adfer opem."* Text is that of *Carmina Illustrium Poetarum Italorum*, III, 78.

[24] Dillingham has followed in part the advice of Sancroft: "As to *lacrymas singultibus urget*—in the penultimate—though the Nightingale hath her sobbe, I know not that any of the chorus have Tears too: Say therefore *Sed dum triste gemens, gemitu singultibus urget* (*Singultus* being more than *gemitus*: and *sic Oratio crescit*)" (BL Sloane 1710, f. 214). Cf. *Fables for Youth* (London, 1777), 14: "Think of your parents so distress'd,/If such the pangs within her breast,/Such pangs yon mourning bird must share,/Such woe, such anguish, and such care" (Fable I: "The Philosopher, Boy and Bird's-Nest," 56-59).

actual title of the whole (*Nemesis a Tergo*), picks up on individual details from the poem itself, and offers some minor changes.[25]

Dillingham's poem tells the legend of the "hangman's stone," a purported tale associated with a milestone in Elton. The legend concerns the stone itself and the strangling of a thief. This has come about by a rather strange set of circumstances: once upon a time a thief stole a sheep, bound its legs together with rope, and then slung the animal upon his shoulders. After carrying the sheep for some time, rather breathless and exhausted, he sat down alongside a milestone and lay back against it. The sheep started to wriggle, and in so doing, managed to droop its feet over the back of the stone, thereby tightening the rope about the thief's neck and eventually strangling him.

The piece achieves a fusion between realism and myth. This is evident in its juxtaposition of precise detail (the location: *finibus Eltonae* [1]; the height of the stone: *pedibus tribus* [3]) with aetiological legend (perhaps the stone was positioned by Mercury, Terminus, or Astraea [6-7]) and folklore (*ut perhibent* [9]). The moral of the whole is aptly conveyed via a series of ironic contrasts. Thus a thief's exultation (*ovans* [12]) is gradually muted by breathlessness (*anhelus* [11]) and exhaustion (*lassus* [16]), and is ultimately silenced by strangulation itself. And that strangulation (*adstrinxit* [20]) is in effect a grimly distorted re-enactment of the thief's treatment of the sheep (*strinxit* [11]), which he bound together and slung upon his shoulders. Hence the moral of the story.

At first glance it would seem that Dillingham's poem, rather like the *Avicula*, draws on the classical tradition to emphasize the moral that retribution is inevitable. To some degree this is indeed true. After all, the theft of an animal and the subsequent punishment incurred by the thief is a theme that seems to trace its origins back to Homer's *Odyssey*, in which Odysseus's crew steals and subsequently devours the oxen of the sun, a crime for which they are punished by a severe storm.[26] Likewise in Homeric Hymn 4, Hermes steals the cattle of the gods. His theft is witnessed by an unnamed old man, in return for whose silence Hermes promises him a good crop of grapes. The old man, however, reports the theft to Apollo.[27] The theft of Apollo's cattle by Hermes also occurs in Hesiod's *The Great Eoiae*. Interestingly, the theft is now associated with

---

[25] Sancroft to Dillingham, 16 Nov 1677 (BL Sloane 1710, f. 214): "Dear Friend, I am much pleas'd with your Thief taken in the Marmor. But what if you should add ... *sive Nemesis a Tergo*?"

[26] Homer, *Odyssey* 1. 7-8; 12. 260-388.

[27] *Homeric Hymn* 4.4. 68-212.

a rock or a stone, and the theme of retribution is prominent. Again there is a witness, in this instance Battus; again his silence is purchased by the promise of a reward. But Hermes returns in disguise to test Battus, offering him a robe if he will tell of any stolen cattle he has seen. Battus succumbs and is punished by being turned into stone.[28] Hesiod's version is closely followed by Ovid in *Metamorphoses* 2. 676-707. Here Apollo's cattle are spied by Mercury, who drives them off and hides them in the woods (*arte sua silvis occultat abactas [boves]* [686]). Battus notices the theft and is bribed by Mercury to keep silent. Battus replies that sooner will a stone tell of the theft than he (*"lapis iste prius tua furta loquetur"/et lapidem ostendit* [696-697]). Mercury returns in disguise and promises Battus a bull and its mate. Battus gives in. Mercury catches him out and turns his faithless heart into flint (*periuraque pectora vertit/in durum silicem* [705-706]). The rock bears the shameful mark of the deed (*qui nunc quoque dicitur index,/inque nihil merito vetus est infamia saxo* [706-707]). And the theme likewise occurs in the story of Hercules and Cacus in Virgil, *Aeneid* 8. Once again the role of the rock is highlighted but now this is interestingly coupled with the theme of strangulation and an emphasis on retribution. The monstrous Cacus steals Hercules's cattle, hiding them in a cave and shutting them (and himself) in by a huge boulder (*raptos saxo occultabat opaco* [8. 211]). This self-imposed enclosure is effected as Cacus breaks a chain and lets a huge rock fall (*deiecit saxum, ferro quod et arte paterna/pendebat* [8.226-227]) thereby making the doorposts impassable. But the secret is disclosed when one of the cattle lows. Hercules grabs a pinnacle of rock and wrenches it from its roots. Cacus becomes trapped in a hollow rock (*inclusumque cavo saxo* [8. 248]) and is eventually twisted by Hercules into a knot, choked and strangled (*hic Cacum .../corripit in nodum complexus, et angit inhaerens/elisos oculos et siccum sanguine guttur* (8. 259-261). Hercules emerges as the *maximus ultor* (8. 201).

But if the subject matter and to some degree the methodology of *Nemesis a Tergo* have some basis in classical poetry, the piece is much more strikingly rooted in a contemporary English world and that world's associated folklore. For the legend at the heart of the poem reflects folklore that attended (and continues to attend) several similar "hangman's stones" in a variety of districts in England. In the late eighteenth century, for example, Samuel Rudder describes a stone and its associated tale as it existed in the parish of Preston:

---

[28] See *The Great Eoiae* 16 in *Hesiod: The Homeric Hymns and Homerica*, trans. H.G. Evelyn-White (Cambridge, Mass., 1977).

> This parish [Preston] is bounded to the westward by the *Irminstreet*, one of the Roman ways passing thro' Cirencester; and at the distance of two miles from the town, but in this parish, there stands an antient, rude stone, about four feet high, lately painted and mark'd as a mile stone. This is vulgarly called Hangmans stone because, it is said, a fellow resting a sheep thereon, (which he had stolen, and tied its legs together for the convenience of carrying it) was there strangled, by the animal's getting its legs round his neck in struggling.[29]

Other such stones are attested by several nineteenth-century contributors to *Notes and Queries*: one in the parish of Foremark, Derbyshire;[30] another "at the end of Lamber Moor, on the roadside between Haverfordwest and Little Haven, in the county of Pembroke,"[31] another "five miles from Sidmouth, on the road to Colyton,"[32] another near the

---

[29] Samuel Rudder, *A New History of Gloucestershire. Comprising the Topography, Antiquities, Curiosities* (Cirencester, 1779), 606. He continues with the following skeptical remark: "But this does not account for the stone's being placed there, and considering the common propensity of inventing stories to obviate names and things not generally understood, I have sometimes been of opinion that all this is fiction, and that the right name of the stone is *Hereman-stone*, so called, like the Roman way upon which it stands, from *Hereman*, a *soldier*; and that the stone is an antient monument for some military person."

[30] See C.S. Greaves, "Churchdown: Similar Legends at Different Places," *Notes and Queries*, 1 (January 5, 1856), 15-16, at 15: "When I was a youth, there were two fields in the parish of Foremark, Derbyshire, called the Great and the Little Hangman's Stone. In the former there was a stone, five or six feet high, with an indentation running across the top of it, and there was a legend that a sheepstealer, once upon a time having stolen a sheep, had placed it on the top of the stone, and that it had slipped off and strangled him with the rope with which it was tied, and that the indentation was made by the friction of the rope caused by the struggles of the dying man."

[31] See J.W. Phillips, "Similar Legends at Different Places," *Notes and Queries* 14, (April 5, 1856), 282: "At the end of Lamber Moor, on the roadside between Haverfordwest and Little Haven, in the county of Pembroke, there is a stone about four feet high called 'Hang Davy Stone,' connected with which is a tradition of the accidental strangling of a sheepstealer, similar to the legend mentioned by Mr. Greaves with reference to the stone at Foremark."

[32] N.S. Heineken, "The Hangman-stone," *Notes and Queries* 1 (May 17, 1856), 402: "It may be interesting to your correspondent Mr. J. W. Phillips, to be informed that at about five miles from Sidmouth, on the road to Colyton, on the right hand side of the road, and near Bovey House, is a large stone known by the name of 'Hangman's Stone.' The legend is precisely similar to that noticed by Mr. Phillips ... and by Mr. Greaves."

north-western boundary of the parish of Littlebury, in Essex,[33] another between Brighton and Newhaven,[34] another between Sheffield and Barnsley.[35] A variation on the legend is provided by a certain Potter in vernacular verse. Now the sheep is replaced by a hart and the thief named as one John of Oxley:

> One shaft he drew on his well-tried yew,
>   And a gallant hart lay dead;
> He tied its legs, and he hoisted his prize,
>   And he toil'd over Lubcloud brow.
> He reach'd the tall stone, standing out and alone,
>   Standing then as it standeth now;
> With his back to the stone he rested his load,
>   And he chuckled with glee to think
> That the rest of his way on the down hill lay
>   And his wife would have spiced the strong drink.

....

---

[33] See Braybrooke, "Hangman Stones," *Notes and Queries* 1 (May 31, 1856), 435: "Some years ago there was still to be seen in a meadow belonging to me, situate near the north-western boundary of the parish of Littlebury, in Essex, a large stone; the name of which, and the traditions attached to it, were identical with those recorded by your correspondents treating of 'Hangman Stones.'

This stone was subsequently removed by the late Mr. Jabez Gibson to Saffron Walden, and still remains in his garden at that place. I have a strong impression that other 'hangman Stones' are to be met with elsewhere, but I am unable to point out the exact localities."

[34] H.E.C., *Notes and Queries* 1 (May 31, 1856), 435-436: "On the right side of the road, between Brighton and Newhaven (about five miles, I think, from the former place) is a stone designated as above, and respecting which is told the same legend as that which is quoted by Henry Keasington."

[35] See Alfred Gatty, "Hangman Stones," *Notes and Queries* 1 (June 21, 1856), 502-503: "At a picturesque angle in the road betwixt Sheffield and Barnsley, and about three miles south of the latter place, there is a toll-bar called 'Hangman-Stone Bar.' Attached to this title is the usual legend of a sheep-stealer being strangled by the kicking animal, which he had slung across his shoulders, and which pulled him backwards as he tried to climb over the stone wall enclosure with his spoil. I do not know that any particular stone is marked as the one on which the sheep was rested for the convenience of the thief in trying to make his escape, but the Jehu of the now extinct Barnsley mail always told this story to any inquiring passenger who happened to be one of five at top—as quaint a four-in-hand as you shall see. I have little doubt that the story told by the 'Jehu,' which my memory may have embellished a little, as is not unusual with travellers' recollections, was the one to which I listened as one of the five outsiders, and in answer to my question the country boys used to insist upon it in my young days that *stones grew*. It seems to me probable that a very moderate monolith may have grown in my recollection to 'a handsome marble column,' and that 'the lord of the manor' was my own phrase rather than our coachman's."

> A swineherd was passing o'er great Ives' Head,
>   When he noticed a motionless man;
> He shouted in vain—no reply could he gain—
>   So down to the grey stone he ran.
> All was clear. There was Oxley on one side the stone,
>   On the other the down hanging deer:
> The burden had slipp'd, and his neck it had nipp'd;
>   He was hanged by his prize—all was clear.[36]

In short *Nemesis a Tergo*, like several of Dillingham's other Latin poems, achieves a subtle fusion of the classical and the contemporary. While the theme, the linguistic medium of neo-Latin coupled with the moralizing personification of Nemesis[37] would seem at first glance to look back to a tradition rooted in the world of ancient Greece and Rome, the legend and the moral of that legend are located in the prevailing and enduring folklore pertaining to the English countryside and its associated landscape.

---

[36] Potter, *Churnwood*, 179, as quoted in C.S. Greaves, "Churchdown: Similar Legends at Different Places," 15.

[37] For other moralizing treatments of Nemesis by neo-Latin poets, see Andreas Alciato, *Illicitum non sperandum*: *Spes simul, et Nemesis nostris altaribus adsunt:/Scilicet ut speres non nisi quod liceat* (*Carmina Illustrium Poetarum Italorum* I, 71); Caelius Calcagninus: *Nemesis*: *Sum Nemesis, hominum cubitores metior omnes,/Neve quis abscedet limite, frena gero* (*Carmina Illustrium Poetarum Italorum* III, 78); Andreas Dactius, *Nemesis*: *Qui mare, qui terram, quique aera miscuit igni,/Terrificans animos peste, cruore, fame:/Pendulus, exustus, vento iactatus et undis;/Praeda iacet terrae, et aeri et igni et aquae* (*Carmina Illustrium Poetarum Italorum* IV, 8).

Chapter 4

A Horticultural Metamorphosis: *Sepes Hortensis*

Dillingham's recreation of natural landscape and of its inhabitants manifests itself on a rather different level in his *Sepes Hortensis*. For this is a poem that celebrates the reinvention of a whole series of creatures from the natural world, and it does so by means of a garden topiary. A draft of the piece was sent by Dillingham to his longtime friend and critic, William Sancroft, who, despite offering a couple of suggestions for improvement,[1] conveyed more than his customary enthusiasm:

> The Truth is, I ought in justice to step yet further back; and to thank you also for your former Letter, and what came with it, your elegant Description of a Garden-hedge, and gravell walk. I will not tell you, how often, and with how much Delight I have pac'd it over from End to End, and entertain'd myself in it.[2]

For Sancroft the poem comes to life, providing an entertaining space that is both literary and pseudohorticultural, a space within whose confines the reader may pace with pleasure. As Ross remarks "gardens are at once parts of the real world–actual pieces of land–and also virtual worlds–coherent sets of possible stimuli."[3] These real and virtual worlds coalesce in Dillingham's poem as a seventeenth-century garden becomes the site

---

[1] "I shall rather take the manly Freedom which you have so often allow'd me, that I am now well-nigh in case to prescribe it. And though you have not made me your Gardiner, nor expressly put the sheers into my Hand; yet I shall take it for granted, that I have your leave to tell you (whether I mistake, or not, of which you are sole judge) that there is a sprig or two in your Hedge which have not the Smoothness, and eveness which so visibly beautifies all the Rest" (BL Sloane 1710, f. 212).

[2] BL Sloane 1710, f. 212.

[3] See Stephanie Ross, *What Gardens Mean* (Chicago, 1998), 176. Cf. Victoria Emma Pagán, *Rome and the Literature of Gardens* (Duckworth, 2006), 2.

of myth and metamorphosis. And more than that, for, as noted below, this "garden hedge" also comes to function as a symbol of transformation and transgression, a locus in which boundaries may be crossed. Or in the words of Foucault:

> The limit and the transgression depend on each other for whatever density of being they possess: a limit could not exist if it were absolutely uncrossable and, reciprocally, transgression would be pointless if it merely crossed a limit composed of illusions and shadows.[4]

The *Sepes Hortensis* was also deemed by Dillingham to be appropriate for much younger eyes than those of an Archbishop. On 14 February 1672, he sent the poem to Justinian Isham for his son Thomas, writing: "I send your sonne a verse made upon a garden clipt hedge which I have sometimes seen."[5] And the event was recorded by the young Thomas in his famous Latin diary: "John Fisher returned from Oundle bringing a letter to my father from Dr Dillingham with some verses on the topiary art."[6] It is possible that Dillingham was aware of Thomas's apparent predilection for hedges and gardens, a predilection that seems to be attested by several of the diary entries.[7] Or his sending the poem may reflect a more general interest in the younger Isham's education. In the same letter Dillingham had recommended a range of texts that might prove useful to the boy's classical studies. Even so his own piece is rather self-consciously juxtaposed with such texts as though assuming a proud place alongside the classics.

After all, the very craft of topiary[8] traces its origins back to the classical world. It was a skill that had developed as a by-product of the Romans' mastery of the technique of pruning. Originally the role of the

---

[4] Michel Foucault, *Language, Counter-Memory, Practice: Selected Essays and Interviews*, trans. D.F. Bouchard and Sherry Simon (Ithaca, 1977), 34.

[5] *The Diary of Thomas Isham of Lamport*, n. 19.

[6] *The Diary of Thomas Isham of Lamport*, 85.

[7] Cf. *The Diary of Thomas Isham of Lamport*, 63: "18 Nov. 1671: Father and I went into the fields to determine where ditches should be dug and hedges planted;" "23 Nov. 1671: Cook went to Olney to buy all kinds of trees to plant in our new orchard"; "24 Nov 1671: The trees were planted in rows in the orchard"; 67: "30 Nov 1671 White [= Robert] pruned the hanging branches which were causing trouble to the fruit trees."

[8] See, in general, Margaret Baker, *Discovering Topiary: The History and Cultivation of Clipped Hedges and Trees* (Hertshire, 1969).

topiarius was one of clipping hedges (*nemora tonsilia*).[9] Thus "the Gardeners, from clipping and laying out every thing by the Line, and turning Trees and Hedges into various Forms, were called *Topiarii*."[10] Gradually the term *opus topiarium* was used to describe the crafted art of the landscape gardener.[11] The skill of the topiary worker was held in high esteem by the ancients,[12] characterized as it was by precision and versatility. As Lawson remarks, the classical topiarist "was not content to depict individual figures but achieved elaborate compositions, such as hunting scenes and naval battles."[13] Pliny the Younger could boast that his Tuscan estate possessed a terraced formal garden with box hedge topiary, from which there sloped a bank with more box hedges clipped into the figures of animals (*bestiarum effigies*).[14] John Ray defined the art as follows: *Topiarium opus vocant arbores et herbas egregio artificio in formas animalium aut aliarum rerum ductas*, and proceeded to emphasize the importance of the vegetation's "flexibility" as it is molded into a variety of shapes (*frutices aut arbusculae tonsiles religatae ... torquentur, flectunturque ad fingenda quae ludunt rerum et animalium argumenta*)[15] quite literally at the hands of an artist of sorts.

---

[9] See Linda Farrar, *Ancient Roman Gardens* (Sutton Publishing, 1998), 161.

[10] Robert Castell, *The Villas of the Ancients* (London, 1728), 118.

[11] See Farrar, *Ancient Roman Gardens*, 161.

[12] Farrar, *Ancient Roman Gardens*, 161: "Topiarii seem to have been held in some regard and comments found in the letters of Cicero reveal aspects of their work that produced admiration."

[13] James Lawson, "The Roman Garden," *Greece and Rome* 19.57 (1950), 97-105, at 104.

[14] *demissus inde pronusque pulvinus, cui bestiarum effigies invicem adversas buxus inscripsit* (*Epist.* 5.6.16).

[15] John Ray, *Historia Plantarum Generalis, Species Hactenus Editas Aliasque Insuper Multas Noviter Inventas et Descriptas Complectens* (London, 1693-1704), I, Index. Cf. Pliny the Elder, *Historia Naturalis* 12.5: *in terram adeo curvantur ut annuo spatio infigantur novamque sibi progeniem faciant circa parentem in orbem quodam opere topiario*. Text is that of Pliny, *Historia Naturalis*, ed. and trans. A.E. Pépin (Paris, 1947). Cf. John Evelyn, *Silva or a Discourse of Forest-Trees* (York, 1786), 239: "The Withy is a reasonably large tree ... the very peelings of the branches being useful to bind arbor-poling, and in topiary works, vineyards, espalier-fruit, and the like: And we are told of some that have been twisted into ropes of an hundred and twenty paces."

Such flexibility and elaboration, which might be regarded by some as an "overemphasis on topiary,"[16] became the hallmark of its medieval and Renaissance counterparts in both Italy and England, as the whole was developed to an unprecedented degree. And this works on both a literary and topographical level. An elaborate topiary garden features prominently in "The Pastime of Pleasure" by Stephen Hawes (c. 1475-1511):

> Then in we went / to the gardyn gloryous
> Lyke to a place / of pleasure moost solacyous
> With flora paynted / and wrought curyously
> In dyvers knottes / of mervaylous gretenes
> Rampande Lyons / stode up wonderfly
> Made all of herbes / with dulcet swetenes
> With many dragons / of mervaylous lykenes
> Of dyvers floures / made full craftely
> By flora couloured / with colours sundry (2008-2016)[17]

A detailed and quasi-ekphrastic description of an "opera topiaria" is included in *Hypnerotomachia Poliphili* (1499),[18] a hugely influential work adapted in England by Robert Dallington in his *Hypnerotomachia: The Strife of Love in a Dreame* (1592). Here shrubbery is trimmed into the shapes of birds, oxen, and dolphins "with their gilles lyke leaves, and their Finnes and their extreame partes of a foliature" to constitute "a Topiarie worke."[19]

But far from being confined to the world of literary fiction, the topiary garden in its most intricate form was very much a part of the real fifteenth-century Italian world. One such garden possessed topiary in the form of ships, galleys, temples, vases, urns, giants, men, women, heraldic

---

[16] Lawson, "The Roman garden," 104.

[17] Text is that of Stephen Hawes, *The Pastime of Pleasure*, ed. W.E. Mead (London: Early English Text Society, 1928).

[18] *Hypnerotomachia Poliphili* (Venice, 1499), chapter 24, 369-370. See, in general, Liane Lefaivre, *Leon Battista Alberti's Hypnerotomachia Poliphili: Re-Cognizing the Architectural Body in the Early Italian Renaissance* (Cambridge, Mass., 1995). Lefaivre's attribution of this anonymous work to Alberti has been contested by recent scholarship. Francesco Colonna "is now believed beyond reasonable doubt to be the author" (*Oxford Companion to Italian Literature*, eds. Peter Hainsworth and David Robey [Oxford, 2002], sv Colonna).

[19] Robert Dallington, *Hypnerotomachia: The Strife of Love in a Dreame* (London, 1592), 50-51. See L.E. Semler, "Robert Dallington's *Hypnerotomachia* and the Protestant Antiquity of Elizabethan England," *Studies in Philology* 103.2 (2006), 208-241.

lions, dragons, centaurs, putti, horses, asses, oxen, dogs, stags, birds, jousters, philosophers, and even a pope and a cardinal.[20] Likewise Maphaeus Barberini sings the praises of an Italian topiary garden in which myrtle trees have been skillfully pruned into the shape of wild animals:

> Hic frutices crescunt, frondes ibi germinat arbos:
> En illic flores, veris odora cohors.
> Tonsilis herba refert, Eoum inventa, tapetes,
> Et myrtus varias ingeniosa feras.[21]

And Renaissance England could boast of her equivalents. Thus Henry VIII's royal retreat Nonsuch was extolled in 1598 by Paul Hentzner for its parks abounding in deer, and its gardens and groves adorned with topiary (*horti delicati, luci topiario opere exornati*).[22] Hampton Court was described in 1599 in the following laudatory terms:

> There were all manner of shapes, men and women, half man and half horse, sirens, serving-maids with baskets, French lilies and delicate crenellations all round made from dry twigs bound together and the aforesaid ever green quick-set shrubs, or entirely of rosemary, all true to life, and so cleverly and amusingly interwoven, mingled and grown together, trimmed and arranged picture-wise that their equal would be difficult to find.[23]

The gardens at Wresehill Castle in Yorkshire were praised by John Leland:

---

[20] See, in general, Alessandro Perosa, *Giovanni Rucellai ed il suo Zibaldone* (London, 1960), 22; Claudia Lazzaro, *The Italian Renaissance Garden* (New Haven and London, 1990); Jennifer Nevile, "Dance and the Garden: Moving and Static Choreography in Renaissance Europe," *Renaissance Quarterly* 52.3 (Autumn 1999), 805-836, at 809.

[21] *Felicitatis Humanae Fuga Coelestis Adeptio*, 25-28. Text is that of *Carmina Illustrium Poetarum Italorum*, II, 45.

[22] *Aedes vero ipsas sic circumcingunt vivaria damnis referta, horti delicati, luci topiario opere exornati, areolae et ambulacra sic arboribus obumbrata ut non aliam sibi sedem ipsa Amoenitas, ubi cum Salubritate una cohabitet, delegisse videatur.* Text is that of Paul Hentzner, *A Journey into England in the Year MDXCVIII* (Twickenham, 1757), 83.

[23] See Roy Strong, *The Renaissance Garden in England* (London, 1979), 33. Cf. William Camden, *Britannia: Or a Chorographical Description of Great-Britain and Ireland* (London, 1735), 164: "But the additions made to it [Hampton Court] by king William and queen Mary, do so far excel what it was before ... The gardens are also improv'd to a wonderful degree, not only in the walks both open and close, and the great variety of topiary-works, but with green-houses, having stoves under them."

> The garde robe yn the castelle was excedingly fair. And so wer the gardeins withyn the mote, and the orchardes withoute. And yn the orchardes were mountes *opere topiario* writhen about with degrees like turninges of cokilshilles to cum to the top without payn.[24]

According to William Marshall "in the days of [John] Evelyn ... topiary work was the Gardener's idol,"[25] while William Lawson could proudly proclaim:

> Your gardeners can frame your lesser wood to the shape of men armed in the field ready to give battell, or swift running Grey Hounds to chase the Deere, or hunt the Hare.[26]

In his 1625 essay "Of Gardens" Francis Bacon sheds some insight upon the complex nature of the art:[27]

> For the Ordering of the Ground, within the Great Hedge, I leave it to Variety of Device; Advising, neverthelesse, that whatsoever forme you cast it into, first it be not too Busie, or full of Worke. Wherein I, for my part, doe not like Images Cut Out in Juniper, or other Garden Stuffe: They be for Children. Little low Hedges, Round, like Welts, with some Pretty Pyramides, I like well: And in some Places, Faire Columnes upon Frames of Carpenter's Worke. I would also, have the Alleys Spacious and Faire. You may have Closer Alleys upon the Side Grounds, but none in the Maine Garden.[28]

---

[24] *The Itinerary of John Leland In Or About the Years 1535-1543*, ed. Lucy Toulmin Smith (London, 1907), I, 53.

[25] William Marshall, *Planting and Ornamental Gardening: A Practical Treatise* (London, 1785), 97.

[26] William Lawson, *A New Orchard or Garden* (London, 1618), ed. Eleanour Sinclair Rohde (London, 1927), 61-65.

[27] For an opposingly negative view of topiary, see, for example, John Evelyn, *Elysium Britannicum*, 97, where armies of topiary figures are described as "lamely and wretchedly represented." See John Dixon Hunt, "Evelyn's Idea of the Garden: A Theory for All Seasons," in *John Evelyn's Elysium Britannicum and European Gardening*, eds. Therese O'Malley and Joachim Wolschke (Washington, 1998), 269-288, at 278-279: "Evelyn resents puerile imitations in gardens or those that have no evident model in the natural world."

[28] Sir Francis Bacon, *The Essayes or Counsels, Civill and Morall*, ed. Michael Kiernan (Oxford, 1985), 139-145, at 142.

His conservative viewpoint is an indication that elaborate topiary was not to everyone's taste. To some degree it anticipates the scorn poured upon the art almost a century later by Alexander Pope:

> How contrary to this Simplicity is the modern Practice of Gardening; we seem to make it our Study to recede from Nature, not only in the various Tonsure of Greens into the most regular and formal Shapes, but even in monstrous Attempts beyond the reach of the Art itself: We run into Sculpture, and are yet better pleas'd to have our Trees in the most awkward Figures of Men and Animals, than in the most regular of their own.[29]

Pope's "Catalogue of Greens" would purport to be the product of "a Virtuoso Gardener who has a Turn to sculpture,"[30] a mock-topiary, as it were, including a representation of "Adam and Eve in Yew, Adam a little shattered by the fall of the tree of Knowledge in the great Storm; Eve and the Serpent, very flourishing."[31] Likewise William Mason in "The English Garden" criticizes topiarists, rebuking the associated Folly and Wealth of those who

>   vainly strove
> By line, by plummer, and unfeeling sheers,
> To form with verdure what the builder form'd
> With stone. Egregious madness; yet pursu'd
> With pains unwearied, with expence unsumm'd,
> And science doating. Hence the sidelong walls
> Of shaven yew; the holly's prickly arms
> Trimm'd into high arcades; the tonsile box
> Wove, in mosaic mode of many a curl,
> Around the fugur'd carpet of the lawn.[32]

Worthy of comparison perhaps is a Latin poem on the gardens of Merton College, Oxford. Here the absence of topiary is extolled. These are gardens that do *not* possess trees pruned in the shape of wild beasts or foliage cut into the shape of letters:

---

[29] Alexander Pope, "On Gardens," *The Guardian* 173 (29 September 1713). Text is that of *The Prose Works of Alexander Pope*, ed. Norman Ault (Oxford, 1936), I, 148.

[30] Alexander Pope, "On Gardens," *The Guardian* 173 (29 September 1713), *Prose Works*, ed. Ault, I, 149.

[31] Alexander Pope, "On Gardens," *The Guardian* 173 (29 September 1713), *Prose Works*, ed. Ault, I, 150.

[32] Text is that of William Mason, *The English Garden* (London, 1777-81), 21-22.

> Non hic factitios habes Leones,
> Nec Pardi modo, Tygridisve rictus,
> Et quas dispositas solent in hortis
> Feras fingere: Quin feras in hortis?
> Nulla in cornua torta belluamque,
> Nulla in literulas secatur herba,
> Nec insignia, Regumve nomen
> Doctus flosculus exprimit, nec ulla
> Gramen tonsile scribitur figura.[33]

But such topiary works as those manifested by Nonsuch continued to be praised. Thus James Dallaway could proclaim of Blenheim: "When Vanbrugh imagined and completed Blenheim, it had little advantage of corresponding scenery, but was deeply inveloped in formal plantations, labyrinths, and topiary works of box and yew."[34]

Although the topiary garden in Dillingham's poem remains unidentified, the skill of its achievement is certainly undeniable. The piece is pervaded by the theme of wonder: by the miraculous art of topiary itself (*cultae ... miracula sepis* [7]; *mira ... arte* [10]), the ecphrastic nature of which is exemplified by the poem as a whole, and explicitly highlighted in the closing lines. For both the topiarist and the poet can give life to the inanimate. As Myers has convincingly argued, "gardens can parallel the skill of the literary author in the design and disposition of his or her material in the composition of a work of literature."[35] Thus perhaps landscape gardening can function as an iconographical mirror of the poetic imagination. Worthy of comparison is Joseph Addison's frequent use of the trope in his "Pleasures of the Imagination" to describe the poet whose

> Rose-trees, Wood-bines, and Jassamines, may flower together, and his Beds be covered at the same time with Lillies, Violets and Amaranthus. His Soil is

---

[33] Anon., *Hortus Mertonensis*, 25-33, cited by Charles Howard Norfolk, *Historical Anecdotes of Some of the Howard Family* (London, 1769), 121. For an equally negative neo-Latin poem on topiary, see Alexander Pope, "On Gardens," *The Guardian* 173 (29 September 1713), *Prose Works*, ed. Ault, I, 148: *hinc et nexilibus videas e frondibus hortos,/implexos late muros, et moenia circum/porrigere, et latas e ramis surgere turres;/deflexam et Myrtum in Puppes, atque aerea rostra:/in buxisque undare fretum, atque e rore rudentes./parte alia frondere suis tentoria Castris;/ scutaque spiculaque et iaculantia citria Vallos.*

[34] James Dallaway, *Anecdotes of the Arts in England* (London, 1800), 145-146.

[35] See K. Sara Myers, "*Docta Otia*: Garden Ownership and Configurations of Leisure in Statius and Pliny the Younger," *Arethusa* 38 (2005), 103-129, at 105.

not restrained to any particular sett of Plants, but is proper either for Oaks or Mirtles, and adapts it self to the Products of every Climate[36]

or more recently Janet Harrison's equation of topiary and authorship in her poem "The Tall One Isn't Moving":

> No, not since the nineteenth century;
> His elegant form, steeple-wise
> Stalks above chaos and campus litter
> Immaculately suited rose
> Button-holed as firmly
> As his prose enunciates a twitter
> Nasal-formed and clipped as quaintly
> Fashioned topiary releases bushes
> Into flight; spruce a sprivet he sallies
> Forth to battle bibliography,
> Marches, rooted in his perfect form,
> To list and buffet with the winds of time.[37]

After all, Pliny's topiary had even included the actual name of the owner and topiarist.[38] Perhaps for Dillingham also self-conscious artistry can be replicated on a literary level in the poem's resurrection of the language and myths of classical Rome?

Such myths moreover readily take their place within a poem whose opening lines turn to the classical world as a means of highlighting the beauty of the garden and hedge in question. This particular *Hortus* is depicted as taking its place alongside the gardens of Alcinous (2)[39] or

---

[36] Joseph Addison, *Spectator* 418 (30 June 1712), ed. Bond, III, 569. Cf. *Spectator* 411 (21 June 1712) in Bond, ed. III, 535-539. See, in general, A.F. Widmayer, "Mapping the Landscape in Addison's 'Pleasures of the Imagination,'" *Rocky Mountain Review of Language and Literature* 50.1 (1996), 19-29.

[37] *College English* 32.8 (1971), 951.

[38] *Alibi pratulum, alibi ipsa buxus intervenit in formas mille descripta, litteras interdum, quae modo nomen domini dicunt modo artificis* [*Epist.* 5.6.35]. Myers, "Docta Otia," 118, remarks that "such *nemora tonsilia* represent a rather new fashion, introduced, as Pliny the Elder tells us, by Gaius Mattius during the reign of Augustus (*Nat.* 12.13)."

[39] *cum poma Alcinous ... numeraret* (2). Cf. Ovid, *Am.* 1.10.56: *praebeat Alcinoi poma benignus ager*; *Ep. Pont.* 4.2.10: *[quis] poma det Alcinoo?* Text is that of *Ovid: Tristia, Ibis, Ex Ponto, Halieutica, Fragmenta*, ed. S.G. Owen (Oxford, 1963). Cf. Virgil, *Georg.* 2.87: *pomaque et Alcinoi silvae*, and Servius *ad loc*: *Alcinoi silvae pomiferae arbores: nam Alcinous, rex Phaeacum, fuit diligens cultor hortorum unde per eius silvas arbores pomiferas intellegimus*. Text is that of *Servii Grammatici In Vergilii Bucolica et Georgica Commentarii*, ed. George Thilo (Teubner, 1887). On the

Adonis (2)[40] acclaimed by such *veteres ... poetae* (1) as Homer and Ovid respectively. During the Renaissance these two literary gardens were frequently juxtaposed as examples of a horticultural ideal. Thus, "the garden of Alcinous in the *Odyssey* provides a fine example of a classical Greek garden, which resembles the Renaissance garden in certain respects."[41] In particular the abundance of fruit (symbolized by Dillingham in the phrase *cum poma Alcinous ... numeraret* [2]) mirrors perhaps the fact that in Alcinous's garden the fruit grows spontaneously, is gathered without toil, and surpasses in its sweetness that of any human garden.[42] This abundance is replicated on a linguistic level for in the Homeric passage in question, as Beretta points out, "the word 'fruit' is mentioned six times," while "fourteen lines out of twenty-three deal with fruit and six different kinds of fruit are mentioned."[43] Likewise the garden of Adonis (here represented by the phrase *cum ... flores numeraret Adonis* [2]) functioned as a virtual symbol "which later developed into a mythical garden with the same status as the gardens of the Hesperides and Alcinous."[44]

Dillingham's topiarist (perhaps like the poet himself) uses his *ingeniosa manus* (10) in such a way that the whole scene serves to recreate the characters of Ovid's *Metamorphoses* (*Nasonis reduces pulchre mentita figuras* [12]). The relevance of the classical poet and the text itself will become apparent in due course and should be viewed alongside the comments of Beretta in regard to the centrality of the Ovidian text in the Renaissance garden:

> Most of Ovid's characters are turned into stones, plants, or trees, all natural forms that are found in the garden. ... The *Metamorphoses* is full of features of Nature that are not what they seem to be. Not only are people turned into

---

garden of Homer's Alcinous as the prototype of the ideal *hortus*, cf. Fabio Segnio, *De Rure Suo Septimiano: alta domus geminis hinc atque hinc cingitur hortis;/Alcinoum tales non habuisse ferunt.* Text is that of *Carmina Illustrium Poetarum Italorum*, IX, 8.

[40] *cum ... flores numeraret Adonis* (2).

[41] Ilva Beretta, "The World's a Garden": *Garden Poetry of the English Renaissance* (Uppsala, 1993), 18.

[42] See Beretta, "The World's a Garden," 18.

[43] Beretta, "The World's a Garden," 18.

[44] Beretta, "The World's a Garden," 20.

> stones, plants and trees, but also into animals and springs. By alluding to Ovid a feeling of Nature being modified by Art is conveyed.[45]

> The transformation of one matter into another reflects the transformation of Nature by Art; Nature is transformed into natural-looking artificial features through Art.[46]

And the poetry itself performs a rather similar function. Dillingham's verses seem to recall Ovid's account of Thetis's ability to transform herself into 100 shapes (*centum mentita figuras* [*Met.* 11. 253])[47] as a means of escaping her would-be lover Theseus (who does eventually get his way with her, thereby fathering Achilles). In Ovid, such shapes included a bird, a tree, and a tigress.[48] In Dillingham, this transformation of an individual nymph is itself transformed and expanded into an ensuing tableau of various animals, a tableau that nonetheless takes its place in a classical landscape now suddenly resurrected. After all, the Renaissance garden, as Battisti has observed "is a measured and well-ordered model of the universe. ... It assumes the function of a sculpture gallery, a pinacotheka, a horticultural encyclopedia *in vivo* ... and a theatre for fantastic imagination."[49]

In terms of the topiary figures in Dillingham's poem there are five categories: a dog, a lion, a serpent, stags/does, and a hunter. But each of these is depicted as a revivified classical myth or scene that is vibrantly alive in its leafy metamorphosis. Like the topiarist, the poet casts the animal world in its verdant form by juxtaposing such adjectives and nouns as *viridantum ... ferarum* (9), *frondosus Hylax* (12) and *frondeus ... venator* (20). And the leafy bodies in which these figures are cast are represented as living, breathing beings. Thus the dog is barking or, as the speaker asks: *audisne ut frondosus Hylax in limine latrat?* [12]) in a verbatim echo and inversion of Virgil's description (in *Ecl.* 8.107) of a

---

[45] Beretta, "The World's a Garden," 45.

[46] Beretta, "The World's a Garden," 100.

[47] Cf. *et se mentitis superos celasse figuris* (*Met.* 5. 326).

[48] Cf. Ovid, *Metamorphoses* 11. 243-245: *sed modo tu volucris (volucrem tamen ille tenebat),/nunc gravis arbor eras: haerebat in arbore Peleus;/tertia forma fuit maculosae tigridis.*

[49] See Eugenio Battisti, "Natura Artificiosa to Natura Artificialis." *The Italian Garden*, ed. David Coffin (Washington: Dumbarton Oaks Colloquium, 1972), 3-36, at 6.

favorable omen signaling the return of the longed-for Daphnis.[50] Likewise the lion is roaring (*saevire* [14]), but this is no ordinary lion (or roar): this is none other than the Nemean beast waiting to be clubbed by the mighty Hercules (14-15), a favorite theme of the Renaissance topiarist.[51] The snake is hissing (*sibilat* [17]) but it is doing so somewhat grotesquely from a multitude of throats, rearing itself up in fury.[52] The stags are actively tossing their antlers on high (*alte iactantes cornua cervos* [18]), the does are grazing,[53] and the hunter is waiting with baited breath (*expectans inhiansque* [21]) as a Gallic hound threatens a hare from behind (*canis dum Gallicus alte/imminet a tergo lepori* [21-22]). The description recalls a simile used by Ovid to convey Apollo's relentless pursuit of Daphne (*ut canis in vacuo leporem cum Gallicus arvo/vidit, et hic praedam pedibus petit, ille salutem* [*Met.* 1.533-534]) and the echo is highly appropriate. For Daphne herself would ultimately be transformed into a laurel tree, its bark encasing her heart, its foliage replacing her hair, its branches now functioning as her arms (*Met.* 1. 548-552) as the swift-footed runner is literally rooted to the spot.[54] It is a stunning metamorphosis whereby in typically Ovidian fashion the human body is usurped by and eventually becomes greenery.[55] Perhaps then

---

[50] *nescio quid certe est, et Hylax in limine latrat* (*Ecl.* 8. 107).

[51] *hic Nemeae videas iterum saevire leonem;/hic iterum ad partes Alcidae clava recurrit* (14-15). Cf. *et vastum Nemeae sub rupe leonem* (*Aen.* 8.295). On the labors of Hercules as a typical theme in the Italian Renaissance garden, see Beretta, "The World's a Garden," 71.

[52] *quin et in adversum non unis faucibus Hydra/sibilat insurgitque furens* (16-17). Cf. *saucius at serpens sinuosa volumina versat/arrectisque horret squamis et sibilat ore/arduus insurgens* (*Aen.* 11.753-755). With Dillingham's account of the serpent hissing *non unis faucibus* (16), cf. Virgil's description of Cerberus at *Aen.* 6. 421: *ille fame rabida tria guttura pandens*.

[53] *damasque arborei tondentes iugera campi* (19). Cf. Lucretius, *De Rerum Natura* 2.660: *tondentes gramina campo*. Text is that of *Titi Lucreti Cari De Rerum Natura Libri Sex*, ed. Cyril Bailey (Oxford, 1963), I. Cf. Ovid, *Am.* 3.15.12: *campi iugera*.

[54] *vix prece finita torpor gravis occupat artus:/mollia cinguntur tenui praecordia libro,/in frondem crines, in ramos bracchia crescunt;/pes modo tam velox pigris radicibus haeret,/ora cacumen habet: remanet nitor unus in illa* (Ovid, *Met.* 1. 548-552).

[55] Cf. the metamorphosis of Cypress into a tree at *Met.* 10. 136-140: *iamque per immensos egesto sanguine fletus/in viridem verti coeperunt membra colorem/et modo qui nivea pendebant fronte capilli,/horrida caesaries fieri sumptoque rigore/sidereum gracili spectare cacumine coelum*.

topiary itself can recreate those Ovidian metamorphoses as indeed can the artist describing such topiary. Prefaced to his poem "The Loves of the Plants" is an interesting statement by Erasmus Darwin:

> Whereas P. Ovidius Naso, a great Necromancer in the famous Court of Augustus Caesar, did by art poetic transmute Men, Women, and even Gods and Goddesses, into Trees and Flowers: I have undertaken by similar art to restore some of them to their original animality, after having remained prisoners so long in their respective vegetable mansions.[56]

Something of this methodology lies at the heart of Dillingham's poem as the leafy dwellers in those "vegetable mansions" transgress the boundaries in which they are confined, thereby achieving some form of poetic liberation. This topiary comes to life as an ecphrasis eventually epitomized by the same phrase (*cernere erat* [26]) used by Virgil to summarize the scenes in the center of Aeneas's shield.[57] And it does so despite or perhaps because of careful signposting (*hic ... videas* [14] ... *hic videas* [18]),[58] balanced syntax (*hic ... iterum/hic iterum* [14-15]), and the rhetorical language (*en!* [13] ... *en!* [20]) in which it is cast. As the ecphrasis proper comes to a rather breathless conclusion, the riveted speaker asks *singula sed quid ego versu comprendere coner?* (23)[59] and does so after a sudden break in the line (22). The line-break was in fact suggested to Dillingham by Sancroft:

> Or rather, were it to me, I would leave it upon the Cesura at *Lepori*, without any supply at all; which would look (me thinks) as done, not because you knew not how to compleat the Verse, but out of a great judgement as abruptly breaking off that particular Enumeration, with *Singula sed quid ego versu comprendere coner?* I am sure Virgil leaves many such half verses, where a seeming defect is not so significative, or at least not visibly to me.[60]

The indeterminacy of the poem's conclusion serves perhaps to encapsulate the inability of language, of art, to confine its subject—a

---

[56] Text is that of D.N. Smith, *The Oxford Book of Eighteenth Century Verse* (Oxford, 1936), 681.

[57] Cf. *Aeneid* 8. 675-676: *in medio classis aeratas, Actia bella,/cernere erat*.

[58] Precedent for such signposting is provided on a more extensive level in the description of Aeneas' shield at *Aeneid* 8. 626, 635, 639, 642, 663, 666.

[59] For the designation *singula* to describe the individual scenes on an ecphrasis, cf. *Aen.* 8. 618: *atque oculos per singula volvit*.

[60] BL Sloane 1710, f. 212.

subject that transgresses boundaries that are literary, topographical, and chronological. For now the speaker's attempt to describe in verse the hedge and its amazing animal shapes is explicitly equated with Homer's ecphrastic representation of the arms of Achilles (*quicquid Maeonides armis inscripsit Achillis* [24]) and the account by Hesiod of the shield of Hercules (*Herculis aut clipeo vates Ascraeus* [25]).[61] It is an equation that finds a parallel of sorts in Pliny's description of the topiary garden on his Tuscan estate, which likewise concludes with a rather self-conscious observation on the way in which his account of this and other aspects of his villa is akin to ecphrastic descriptions by Homer and Virgil of the arms of Aeneas and Achilles:

> Vides quot versibus Homerus, quot Vergilius arma hic Aeneae Achillis ille describat; brevis tamen uterque est quia facit quod instituit. vides ut Aratus minutissima etiam sidera consectetur et colligat; modum tamen servat. non enim excursus hic eius, sed opus ipsum est. (*Epist.* 5.6.43)

Perhaps then Myers's argument that Pliny used his descriptions of an estate as "ecphrastic models of self-representation"[62] is equally applicable to Dillingham himself. As leafy figures undergo a metamorphosis into the personae of classical myth, a seventeenth-century topiary becomes a poetic ecphrasis which reinvents a world that is both classical and contemporary. Such reinvention lies at the heart of Dillingham's original Latin poetry included in the *Poemata Varii Argumenti*. This is neo-Latin verse that "sports" with the classics in such a way that "recreation" is ultimately wedded to timeless recreation.

---

[61] Cf. Ovid, *Am.* 1.15.11: *vivet et Ascraeus*; Virgil, *Georg.* 2.176: *Ascraeumque ... carmen*.

[62] Myers, "*Docta Otia*," 103. Cf. 122: "Pliny's evocation of the tradition of poetic ecphrasis suggests that his villa descriptions may also be read as self-reflective models of the text itself as a work of art."

APPENDIX 1

WILLIAM DILLINGHAM'S LATIN POETRY

LATIN TEXT AND FACING ENGLISH TRANSLATION[1]

BY

ESTELLE HAAN

---

[1] Text is that of *Poemata Varii Argumenti Partim e Georgio Herberto Latine (Utcunque) Reddita, Partim Conscripta a Wilh. Dillingham, S.T.D.* (London, 1678). I have modernized spelling and punctuation.

Suleianum
Ad Illustrissimum Carolum
Westmorlandiae Comitem

Accipe, Magne Comes, Tibi debita Carmina, Musae
    Idem materies ingeniumque meae

Aufonias propter ripas, qua cogitur unda
ferre iugum et famam debet Wansfordia ponti,
silvae contiguus modicique cacumine montis,
est locus Australem qui partem versus et ortum
vallesque villasque et longos prospicit agros.   5
Terra olim agricolae duros experta labores,
at postquam cincta est vivae munimine sepis
et viridi donata toga de cespite puro,
tota vacat ludo magnis celebranda triumphis,
miraturque novos aurata veste colonos.   10
hanc bene detonsam ac ad vivum cespite raso
levigat atque polit subigitque volubile saxum,
labentem sphaeram ne qua fetusca moretur.
    Huc generosa cohors animo depellere curas
quum iuvat et sudum est dictis plerumque diebus   15
convolat; in partes itur: "tu Guelfius esto;
hic Gibelinus erit, furiis tamen ante remotis,
quin et avaritia: turpes haec suscitat iras.
sed neque pro nuda iubeo te laude pacisci:
'exacuit modicum; nimio si pignore certes,   20
corrumpis ludum ne sit sincera voluptas.'
laudo tamen veterum ritus qui munera bina
praemia victori statuunt, solatia victo.
    Heus puer! huc propere sphaeras splendore coruscas
expedias, lateri immissum quas fusile plumbum   25
et docuit solidare gradus et ducere gyros."
stat iuxta domus exilis, gratissima fessis
umbra viris; eadem ludentibus arma ministrat.
hinc puer expromit sphaeras, hic nocte recondit.
    Primus ibi ante omnes in arenam Sylvius heros   30
descendit, multa virtute insignis et arte,
seu circumducto metam contingere gyro,
sive per hostiles opus est perrumpere turmas.
is (postquam limen signarat lamina ferri)
protinus emittit nullo molimine sphaeram   35
exiguam. haec Helena est, cursus haec meta futuri;
hanc ambire omnes: felix qui limine primo
egressus tandem illius requiescit in ulnis.
tum sphaeram dextra complexus lumine certo
signat iter, prono veneratur corpore Nympham,   40
effunditque globum, tacito qui flumine lapsus

Appendix 1

Sulehay
To the Most Distinguished Charles,
Earl of Westmorland

Receive, eminent Earl, poetry that is your due,
you who are both the subject and the inspiration of my Muse.

Close to the banks of Avon where the stream is forced to bear the yoke, and Wansford owes its fame to a bridge, near a wood and on the top of a hillock there is a place which, facing in the direction of the south and the east, commands a prospect of valleys, villages, and distant fields. In times past this land experienced the severe toils of the farmer, but after being encircled by the protection of a quick-set hedge and endowed with a green toga of smooth turf, it is completely free for sport, worthy to be celebrated in mighty triumphs as it marvels at its new cultivators in gear of gold. When this has been properly sheared, with its turf naturally trimmed, a stone roller levels, smoothens, and polishes it in case at any point a clump of grass might check the progress of the gliding bowl.

To this spot there flocks a band of gentry when it is their wish to dispel anxieties from their mind, when the weather is clear, and mostly on prescribed days. They divide into sides: "You be Guelfo; this one will be Gibelinus, but banish beforehand madness and greed as well: this stirs up shameful anger. Still, neither do I enjoin you to strike a bargain for nothing but renown: 'that which is small acts as an incentive; but if you compete for a stake that is excessive, you spoil the sport with the result that the pleasure is not genuine.' Nonetheless I commend the customs of the ancients, which establish two rewards: prizes for the victor, consolation prizes for the vanquished.

Come on, boy! Fetch here quickly the resplendently gleaming bowls taught by the molten lead poured into their side both how to steady their pace and how to move in circles." Close by is a little house, a most welcome shade for the weary men. This same place supplies arms for the sportsmen. It is from here that the boy brings out the bowls; it is here that he stores them at night.

Then first of all there comes down into the arena Sylvius the hero, renowned for his great bravery and skill, whether the need be to make contact with the jack in circular formation or to burst through the enemy squadrons. Once the iron marker had indicated the starting-point, immediately and effortlessly he casts forth a tiny ball. This is Helen: this is the goal for the path of subsequent bowling: it is she who is encircled by all; happy is he who leaves the starting-point and rests at last in her arms. Next grasping a bowl in his right hand, with unwavering gaze he marks out its course, worships the Nymph with his body prostrate, and shoots forth a bowl. This gliding along like a silent stream,

metae contiguus media requiescit arena.
　Excipit hunc Nisus, quo non praestantior alter,
sive globum versare manu seu stringere metam,
sive hostem turbare loco seu vincere cursu.　　　　　　　　45
hic sphaeram librat, minimi quae conscia plumbi
radit iter laevum interior meliorque priorem
detrudit spatio metaeque amplexibus haeret.
　Tum varius reliquis animus: spes, ira metusque
et pudor et studium laudisque immensa cupido.　　　　　　50
quisque suas partes tutari mente paratus,
sed non quisque ducis laudes virtutibus aequat.
　Hic multum cupiens titulos augere triumphi
atque locum sperans saltem retinere secundum
currentem sphaeram manibus pedibusque fatigat:　　　　　55
nunc festinantem vocis moderatur habena;
ignavum et sine honore globum nunc increpat et mox
consulit, hortatur, laudat; tum corpore torto
evitare docet cautes monitisque videtur
emendasse suis. quid non sibi somnia fingunt?　　　　　　60
　Ille volens capto Nisum detrudere muro
fallitur inque auras vires effundit inanes.
infelix virtus! sed magnis excidit ausis.
　At veluti in castris olim Romana iuventus
induperatori si quando forte peric'lum　　　　　　　　　　65
imminet, extemplo sese ad praetoria sistit,
tutaturque ducem multoque satellite cingit:
haud aliter Nisum socii fido agmine cingunt,
obice firmantes aditus hostemque morantur.
　Quid reliquos memorem, varius quos abstulit error?　　　70
hic praetervectus metam post terga relinquit;
is medio languet, seu carcere segnior exit
seu titubante pede et duplicato tramite vectus.
hic hiat immodice nimiis ambagibus; ille
interiore secat gyro, vel devius errat　　　　　　　　　　　75
averso plumbo tota ridendus arena.
　Sylvius, ut vidit nullum superesse suorum
qui conclamatis posset succurrere rebus,
non animis cadit aut fatis irascitur; atqui
oblatam gaudet qualem sibi posceret ultro　　　　　　　　80
materiem dignamque sua virtute palaestram.
"difficili arguitur praesens ac ardua virtus,
altius opposito surgit velut aggere flumen."
tum spatium omne suo permensus lumine, nunc hos,
nunc illos aditus rimante explorat ocello.　　　　　　　　85
"invia virtuti nulla est via," protinus infit.
　Dixerat et limen repetit sphaeramque poposcit
quam prudens illos olim servarat in usus.
viribus hanc totis intorquet: at evolat illa
fulminea vibrata manu ruptasque phalangas　　　　　　　90
dissipat hostiles, huc, illuc funera spargens;

rests in the middle of the arena close to the jack.

This is followed by Nisus, than whom no other is more outstanding whether in spinning a bowl in his hand or in skimming the jack or in dislodging the enemy from his position or in conquering by running. He balances a bowl, which privy to its lesser quantity of lead, skirts a left-hand path on the inside, and overtaking the previous bowl, it pushes it aside from its place and clings to the embraces of the jack.

Then in the others there arises a variety of emotions: hope, anger, fear, shame, enthusiasm, and a huge passion for glory. Each one is mentally prepared to protect his own side, but not everyone can match with bravery their leader's glory.

This man, longing greatly to increase his claim to triumph, and hoping to hold on to second place at least, doggedly pursues with his hands and feet a bowl as it runs along: now by the reining power of his voice he restrains the bowl as it hurries along; now he rebukes the bowl as lazy and lacking in honor, and next he advises, encourages, praises it; then with bodily contortions he instructs it on how to avoid the rocks, under the impression that he has corrected it by his own advice. What fancies do not dreams produce?

That man, wishing to thrust Nisus down from the wall he has captured, makes a mistake, and pours his strength into thin air: Unlucky bravery! But it is only from mighty exploits that a fall ensues.

But just like young Roman soldiers in their camp in times gone by: if ever danger happens to threaten their general, they immediately station themselves beside his tent and protect their leader, surrounding him with many bodyguards; no differently do his teammates surround Nisus in a loyal band, strengthening the approaches with a barrier, and delaying the enemy.

Why should I tell of the rest who were led astray by mistakes of various kinds? This one, cast too far ahead, leaves the jack behind: another grows torpid in midpath, whether from leaving the starting-post at too sluggish a pace, or whether cast by a bowler with tottering step and borne on a path twice the length. This one is too hesitant amid excessive uncertainty; that one marks a path with an inner circle, or else wanders off course, disadvantaged by the weight of the lead, an object of ridicule in the whole arena.

When Sylvius saw that there were none of his men remaining who could help his lost cause, he did not lose courage or become angry with destiny; instead he was glad that there was presented to him the type of opportunity which he would voluntarily call for—a wrestling-ground worthy of his own bravery: "It is in times of difficulty that the presence of a soaring bravery is proven; just as a river rises higher when a dam is placed in its way." Then, scanning with his gaze the entire space, with the eye of scrutiny he investigates now these approaches, now those. "No path is inaccessible to bravery," he instantly says.

Having spoken, he made for the starting-point once again and demanded a bowl which he had wisely kept in reserve for that very purpose. He hurls this with all his strength: now this, brandished by a hand of thunder, flies out, breaks through and shatters the enemy phalanxes, scattering death on this side and on that,

obiectasque moras cursus molita per omnes,
abducit metam et summa consistit arena.
    Protinus it coelo clamor totusque remugit
mons circum; trepidat mediis exterrita silvis   95
Nympha loquax, dubitans tanti quae causa triumphi
quanto non meminit celebrari funera cervi.
diditur in silvas tonitru, Nymphaeque minores
"Silvius" ingeminant: "ex illo tempore nobis
Silvius inque illis notissima nomina silvis."   100

Campanae Undellenses

Nox hiberna duas prope iam confecerat horas,
cessarantque foris operae clamorque virorum;
nulli tranquillum turbabant aëra venti,
nec coelum audebant nubes temerare serenum,
dum grex stellarum toto pascebat Olympo;   5
candela emicuit sumpsitque domestica regna
aemula solaris radii tenebrasque fugaces
dispergens, horas longe de nocte redemit;
cum procul a Camo veteris novus incola ruris
solus ego en Ferus atque meus consedimus una   10
ante focum, agrestes recitantes ordine musas.
musica sed nostras subito pervenit ad aures,
proxima quam tusis campanis villa ciebat,
et fovit vallis liquidum resonantibus undis
in tantum ut totum complerent aethera cantu.   15
    Tum Ferus, "ah! templum nostros habet illud amores:
o mihi prae cunctis dulcissima musica, quam te
depereo! merita es nostro quoque carmine dici.
    Protinus agnovi veteris vestigia flammae,
qua cultum populumque Dei sacrosque labores   20
arsit dum licuit; sed et ardet et inde revelli
sola morte potest; poterit neque morte revelli."
    Tunc ego: "quin nostros liceat proferre calores
quandoquidem simili nonullus tangor amore.
olim (nam memini) patrii cum ruris alumno   25
grammaticus teneros ludus mihi fingeret annos,
villa exilis erat paucis contenta colonis,
queis tamen harmonicae mentes coelique capaces.
his, si quando labor curvi cessabat aratri,
campanas pulsare sacras erat una voluptas.   30
musica praelongae dabat haec solamina nocti
excivitque novos iam multo mane labores;
illa renascentis cecinit cunabula solis,
nec prius ad mollem vergebant lumina somnum
funera quam clausae fuerant celebrata diei.   35
nulla dies abiit non his cantata Camoenis.

and making its way through all hindrances cast in its path, it removes the jack and comes to rest at the top of the arena.

Immediately shouting issues toward the heavens and the mountain reverberates all about; amid the woods the babbling Nymph trembles in terror, wondering what can be the reason for a triumph the extent of which she does not recall being celebrated even at the death of a stag. The woods are beset with thunder and the lesser Nymphs redouble: "Silvius: from this time Sylvius will be for us and in these woods the most famous name!"

The Bells of Oundle

Winter's night had already completed virtually two hours, and outdoor work and the din of men had come to a halt; no winds disturbed the tranquil air, and clouds did not dare to defile the clear sky as the flock of stars grazed upon the whole of Olympus. There shone forth a candle which, rivaling the sun's ray, took up her regal residence, and dispersing the fleeing darkness, she atoned for the hours of a long night. It was then that I in solitude and far from Cam, a new inhabitant of an ancient countryside, I and (behold) my Wild sat down together before the hearth, reciting in succession our rustic muses. But suddenly there reached our ears music produced by the tolling bells of a village close by, soothing the valleys in clearly resonating waves to such a degree that they filled the entire ether with their song. Then Wild proclaimed: "Ah! That church possesses my love. O music most sweet to me above all else; how I am dying about you! You deserve to be proclaimed in my song too.

I have instantly recognized the traces of the old flame that (when it was permissible) burned with love for worship, for the people of God, and his sacred works; but burning it is still, and only by death alone can it be wrenched from there—in fact, not even by death can it be wrenched from there."

Then I said: "I too can disclose my passion inasmuch as I am touched in no slight degree by a similar love. Once upon a time (for remember it I can) when as a nursling of my native countryside, grammar school was molding my tender years, there was a small village contented in its few inhabitants, who possessed nonetheless minds in harmony and with an apprehension of heaven. Whenever the labor of the curved plough had ceased, their single pleasure was to ring the sacred bells. This music bestowed solace upon night's exceeding length. It summoned new toils when morning was already underway; it sung out the cradle of the reborn sun; and eyes did not incline toward gentle sleep until the funeral of the day's closure had been celebrated. No day passed unsung by these Camoenae:

sic veniente die, sic decedente canebant,
et penitus toto delebant pectore curas.
interea vario mulcebant aethera cantu,
pergratisque sonis vicinia tota sonabat. 40
o illas dulces noctes cum ducere somnum
ad numeros licuit vigilemque revisere vitam!
    Hae mihi deliciae fuerant puerilibus annis.
floruit at postquam tenera lanugine mentum,
grandior Undelae cepit mea pectora cantus, 45
quae tantum villas inter caput extulit omnes
quantum inter corylos umbrosa cacumina quercus.
haec saxo exsurgens vivo, facieque decora
perrarum agnoscit congesto cespite culmen
(ut cui tecta facit de fisso lamina saxo) 50
promissique sedens equitansque in tergore montis,
Aufonias utrinque pedem demittit ad undas,
sed bino e saxis firmat vestigia ponte,
altaque turrigerum caput inter nubila condit.
hic habitant illae Musae dulcesque Camoenae 55
quae circumfusam demulcent carmine vallem.
    Corpore sunt multum diverso quinque sorores
et queis vox pariter dispar: haec tinnit in altum;
illa gravis graviterque canit tonitruque canorum
et circumductos displodit ad aethera bombos. 60
audiit hanc Echo tremuitque in sedibus imis.
credibile est ipsos commotos carmine Manes.
hae curas abigunt, hae purgant faecibus auras,
atque malos abigunt genios (si credere fas sit),
qui simul ac resonant campanae e turribus altis 65
praecipitare fugam, metuentes vota precantum.
sic olim visis servi fugere flagellis
ac sortis memores dominis sua terga dederunt.
    Quam gratum, quam dulce melos, seu tempore sancto
classica sacra canunt seu visum est luce profesta 70
in gyrum glomerare sonos numerisve peritis
ter quadragenos variare ex ordine versus!
his o quis sextam adiiciet? tum nempe liceret
sexcentos variare modos. quis at optimus ille
qui dabit ut centum pulsanti rite quotannis 75
praeconi sacro possint addicere libras?
quisquis erit, meritos illi cernemus honores.
    Hae, quoties Caroli nobis lux festa recurrit,
festinae surgunt multa de nocte sorores
magnaque venturae meditantur fata diei. 80
tum subito gnarique viri iuvenesque periti
in numerum pulsant adductis funibus aera,
protinus et toti dictant sua gaudia ruri.
    Comminus Undelam ac intra lapidem inde secundum
quatuor atque decem circumstant ordine villae, 85
discipulae villae, ac arrectis turribus adstant.

thus they sang as day approached, thus as day departed, and they completely wiped away anxieties from the heart. In the meantime they soothed the air with different types of music and the entire neighborhood used to resound with their very pleasing tones. O those sweet nights when I could fall asleep to their rhythms and when I could awaken to behold life again! These were the delights of my childhood years. But after my chin bloomed with tender down, my heart was captivated by the more serious music of Oundle, which has reared her head as high among all villages as oaks rear their shady summits amid hazel-trees. This, rising out of living stone and of charming aspect, claims as its own an exceptional roof of piled turf (since anyone can make a roof of tiled stone), and sitting and riding upon the back of a projecting mountain, it dips its feet on both sides in the waters of the Avon: but it strengthens its footsteps by two stone bridges and buries its turret-bearing head amid the lofty clouds. This is the dwelling-place of those Muses, the sweet Camoenae, who with their music soothe the surrounding valley.

There are five sisters of very different physical appearance, whose voices are equally different: this one rings on high; that one is ponderous and sings ponderously and with the resonance of thunder as she bursts forth her prolonged booming to the sky. Echo has heard her and has trembled in the depths of her abode. It is to be believed that the very spirits of the underworld have been moved by the music. These drive off anxieties; these purify the breezes of defilements and ward off evil spirits (if there is any credence to the tale) who, as soon as the bells resound from the lofty towers, hasten their flight in fear of the orisons of those at prayer. Thus in times past slaves took to flight upon seeing the whip, and mindful of their lot, they showed their masters their backs.

How pleasing, how sweet is the melody, whether the sacred trumpets sound at a feast day or whether on an ordinary day they seem to concentrate their tones into a circle or with skillful rhythms to alternate thrice forty verses in succession! O who will add a sixth one to these? Then indeed they could alternate six hundred notes. But who is that excellent one who will grant them the ability to add measures to the hallowed herald as it ritualistically strikes one hundred times every year? Whoever it is, we will determine deserved glory for him.

Behold! As often as the festive day of Charles recurs for us, the sisters arise in haste late at night, and they contemplate the mighty destiny of the forthcoming day. Then suddenly experienced men and skillful youths pull the ropes and rhythmically strike the bronze, and instantly they all proclaim their joys to the countryside.

Close to Oundle and within the second milestone from there are situated all about fourteen hamlets in succession, hamlets that act as her pupils, standing by with their steep towers.

hae postquam accepere sonos paulumque moratae,
attonitis similes, taciturno murmure secum
hos recitant intusque canunt et carmina fingunt.
ut sibi prima fides clangunt. tum protinus omne   90
campanile sonat dum tintinnabula cantant,
et totas variis implent tinnitibus auras.
astra micant blandum, reparabilis adsonat Echo.
   At quaedam villa est paulo distantior illis
(villa olim agricolis multis habitata, priusquam   95
—quod mireris—oves dominosque domosque vorarent)
quae turrim attollens sublimem in vertice montis
orditur cantus, sed deficit incola quartus,
pastorisque canis iam solam novit avenam.
   Naiades interea excitae per caerula regna   100
dimidiae exsistunt undis; tum flumina circum
stare iubent, laetis iuvant indulgere choreis.
undae stant minime curantes aequore mergi.
Nymphae partitis operis sua gaudia pandunt:
pars pedibus plaudunt choreas, pars carmina dicunt,   105
quarum quae forma pulcherrima Caliopeia
praecentrixque chori facilisque praeire canendo,
gaudentemque canit populum Regemque reductum.
quin etiam meminisse iuvat pretiosa peric'la
tam cari capitis, quo non est mitior ullus   110
regnantum in terris aut observantior aequi.
tum Carolum toties salvum et miracula narrat,
coelitus ereptum bello trans aequora mittit,
dein revocat repetitque domum redimitque corona
augustos laeta celebrantem pace triumphos;   115
gaudia tum populi memorat laetosque furores.
sed iam senserunt se tintinnabula laetis
incaluisse sonis, nec enim sua gaudia tanta
aera satis capiunt. timor est ne forte liquentur.
   Ilicet ad pontum properato currite, lymphae,   120
iam vos coeperunt avidis deposcere votis
Petropolitani, nudique in litore pisces.
muneris at tanti memores labentibus annis
hanc sibi dilectam lascivo flumine vallem
circumludentes, passus ter mille vagantur   125
Nymphae, dantque suo villae de nomine nomen.
campanae dulces valeant vigeantque, nec unquam
tristia cancrino plangant incendia motu."
   Haec ego campanis super et super aere canoro
hic procul a Musis Cami et procul exsul ab undis,   130
ambit qua Undelae ripas uxorius amnis,
pauca Fero nostro multum nictantibus astris,
dum mea perdulcis declinat lumina somnus.
et cecini et cecinisse iuvat. scit cetera Musa.

After they have heard the tones, hesitating a little as though in a state of wonderment, they recite them to themselves with silent humming, sing them internally and formulate their song. As soon as they have the confidence, they ring out. Then every field immediately resounds as the bells toll, filling every breeze with their varied ringing. The stars gently gleam and Echo, recovering the sound, responds in accompaniment.

But slightly more distant from them there is a hamlet (a hamlet once inhabited by many farmers until—something to make you marvel—sheep devoured both their owners and their homes). This, rearing its tower aloft upon a mountain top begins the song, but its fourth inhabitant falters—the only music familiar to the dog has been that of the shepherd's pipe.

Meanwhile the Naiads are aroused amid their kingdom of blue, and stand halfway up in the water; then they command the rivers all about to stand still. Their wish is to indulge in joyful dancing. The waves stand still, with no concern at all to be mingled with the sea. The Nymphs apportion their tasks and reveal their joys: some beat out the dances with their feet; others sing songs. Calliope, the most beautiful of them in appearance, the leading songstress of the troop, ready to proclaim the song first, sings of a rejoicing people and the restoration of the King. She even takes pleasure in recalling the costly dangers to an individual so beloved, than whom no other monarch on Earth is more gentle or more observant of righteousness. Then she tells of Charles saved so many times, and of miraculous events: after his divine escape from war she sends him across the sea, then summons him back, and fetches him home again, and encircles him with a crown as he celebrates august triumphs in joyful peace. Then she tells of a people's joy and ecstatic happiness. But soon the bells realized that they had become heated by the joyous tones; for their bronze cannot adequately encapsulate joy so great. Their fear is that they may fade into nothingness.

Waters, hastily speed at once to the deep: those who dwell amid the rocks have already begun to ask for you with ardent prayers, as have the fish exposed upon the shore. But as the years slip by the Nymphs, mindful of a service so great, and sporting in a frolicking stream about this, their beloved valley, wander three thousand paces and name the village after their own name. May the sweet bells be strong and flourish, and may they never mourn the grim heat associated with the movement of Cancer."

These few things about bells and about the tuneful bronze I, an exile far from the Muses and far from the waters of the Cam, have sung and am delighted to have sung to my Wild here where the uxorious stream encircles Oundle's river banks, under the ever flickering stars, until a very sweet sleep closed my eyes. The rest the Muse knows.

Avicula

En! viden ut volucris pictis iam florida pennis
(aetheris ignaram cum primum sedula mater
elicit in ramos extremos hospitis ulmi,
qua patriam parvosque lares suspenderat atque
inde audere iubet per inania) pectore toto   5
palpitat, ignoto metuens se credere coelo!
    Hortatu hanc mulcet mater, vanosque timores
arguit exemplo: suadet, iubet, increpat, urget;
tum volat atque redux cessantem corripit; inde
itque reditque viam toties, dum semita trita   10
signet iter liquidum descriptum remige penna.
    Filia maternis monitis commota tenellas
alas saepe levat, prona cervice vocanti
annuit, obsequium blando modulamine spondet.
at quoties passis conatur in aëra pennis,   15
in ramis toties haeret nisusque resorbet.
mox ubi prima fides umeris, evicta pudore
avolat et rudibus vacuum diverberat alis.
    Ante volans mater vicina constitit orno
ut natam exciperet peregrinis sedibus hospes.   20
quam simulac ferri nimio in sublime volatu
vidit, multa timens tremulo stridore reprensat.
heu, frustra! nam tanta illam fiducia pennae
impulit ut nidique metusque oblita prioris,
iam coelum meditetur ovans et cogitet astra.   25
non illam pietas, non illam cura parentis
abstrahere inde potest. fertur; iam iamque videri
desiit, atque immersa polo latet aethere toto.
heu matris gemitus, multum et lacrimabile carmen!
ah quoties, "dilecta, mane, mane, improba," dixit?   30
(dicere vel visa est, latè loca questibus implens)
"quo ruis? ah! nimio miseram ne redde parentem
obsequio; haud fuerat mea iussa capessere tanti."
noxiaque incassum tandem mandata retrectans,
lugubri natam, natam bis voce vocabat,   35
et sua crudeli laniabat pectora morsu.
    Illa volans volitansque, volans volitansque per auras
sublimi scandit cochlea; tum perforat orbes
atque vagos mediis lusus suspendit in astris.
ast ubi languescunt alae viresque fatiscunt,   40
amotasque videt terras coelique profundi
ignotas restare vias, gravis ingruit horror
ebria ne tandem coelo Phoebique sagittis
praecipitata ruat tristesque adigatur ad umbras.
saepe suam matrem non exaudita vocabat   45
et sero neglecta dolet mandata parentis.
sed dum triste gemens luctus singultibus urget,
respiciens terras pronis delabitur alis.

The Little Bird

Look! Do you see how the bird, already adorned with colored plumage (as soon as her painstaking mother has enticed her [though unacquainted with the heavens] onto the furthermost branches of a welcoming elm, where she had hung her homeland and little dwelling, enjoining her to make a daring flight from there through the void) utterly quivers in her heart, fearing to entrust herself to a sky she does not know!

Her mother soothes her with exhortation, and by her own example proves that her fears are in vain: she persuades, commands, rebukes, exhorts; then she flies and returning, she grabs hold of her hesitant offspring; next she proceeds and comes back again upon a path so many times until a well-worn track indicates a clear route marked by the oarage of her wing.

The daughter, stimulated by a mother's advice, often raises her delicate little wings and bending her neck, nods to her as she calls, pledging obedience with charming chirping. But as many times as she makes trial of the air with outstretched wings, so many times does she remain fixed amid the branches, stifling those efforts. Soon placing initial trust in her shoulders and overcome by shame, she flies off and beats at the empty air with inexperienced wings.

Her mother, flying ahead, rests upon a neighboring ash with the intention that it receive her daughter hospitably in a foreign abode. As soon as she sees her borne by a flight that is exceedingly high, she is very afraid and rebukes her with a quavering shriek. In vain, alas! For she is driven on by such confidence in her wing that she forgets her nest and her previous fear, exultantly contemplates the sky and ponders the stars. No sense of duty, no regard for her parent can drag her away from there. She is borne along, and now gradually she ceases to be visible and, immersed in the sky, she lies hidden in the entire heavens. Alas a mother's groaning and her very mournful song! Ah how many times did she say: "My dear, stay; stay, you mischief-maker" (or so she seemed to say, filling the regions far and wide with her plaintive laments). "Where are you rushing to? Ah do not through your over obedience make a parent wretched; carrying out my orders was not worth such a price." Eventually revoking though in vain her injurious instructions, she called for her daughter; for her daughter she called twice with a mournful voice, and tore at her own breast with cruel pecking.

She, flying and fluttering, fluttering and flying through the breezes, climbs in a high spiral; next she penetrates the spheres and in her erratic playfulness hangs suspended amid the stars. But when her wings grow weak and her strength grows weary, she sees that the earth is in the distance while all that remains are the unknown tracts of heaven's heights. A serious dread assails her that in her intoxication for the heavens she might be hurled headlong by the arrows of Phoebus and eventually fall and be thrust down to the gloomy underworld. Often, though unheard, she called for her mother, and all too late regretted that she had disregarded a parent's instructions. But amid her sorrowful moaning and as she plied her lamentations with sobbing, she looks back at the earth, and with wings pointing downwards, down she sinks.

Sepes Hortensis

Hortus erat qualem veteres cecinere poetae
cum poma Alcinous, flores numeraret Adonis;
hic spatia ingenti multum solidata cylindro
praebebat Musae meditanti laevis arena;
margine quam longo pariter utrinque coercent,   5
et pingunt variis habitatae floribus herbae.
at quis tam cultae referat miracula sepis?
quae densas aequata comas in vertice summo
viminea ostentat viridantum armenta ferarum,
ingeniosa manus mira quas luserat arte   10
Nasonis reduces pulchre mentita figuras.
    Audisne ut frondosus Hylax in limine latrat?
en! pecora introitu prohibet puerisque minatur.
hic Nemeae videas iterum saevire leonem;
hic iterum ad partes Alcidae clava recurrit.   15
quin et in adversum non unis faucibus Hydra
sibilat insurgitque furens, reparabile monstrum.
hic videas alte iactantes cornua cervos,
damasque arborei tondentes iugera campi.
frondeus, en, adstat laxis venator habenis,   20
exspectans inhiansque, canis dum Gallicus alte
imminet a tergo lepori.
    Singula sed quid ego versu comprendere coner?
quicquid Maeonides armis inscripsit Achillis,
Herculis aut clipeo vates Ascraeus, id omne   25
illic cernere erat seducto vimine textum;
auctoresque citat rerum vegetabilis ordo.

Nemesis a Tergo

Finibus Eltonae sublimis vertice montis,
Petropolitanas qua semita ducit ad arces,
saxum telluri infixum pedibus tribus exstat
non ingratum equiti, qui per declivia montis
descendisse cupit salva cervice pedester.   5
sive hoc Mercurius posuit seu Terminus olim
sive hoc forte loco terras Astraea reliquit,
ultima non magno signans vestigia saxo.
    Furcifer (ut perhibent) huius malus incola ruris,
olim e vicino pecudum furatus ovili,   10
quadrupedem strinxit, colloque umerisque levavit.
ibat ovans praedam nactus tenebrisque potitus
(hactenus et votis arrisit pulchra Laverna).
non tamen evasit nec furtum impune ferebat.
namque semel clivum quum conscendisset anhelus,   15
hic lassus desedit humi, saxoque reclinans
suffulsit pecudem; quae primum nacta quietem et

A Garden Hedge

There was a garden like that of which ancient poets have sung when Alcinous counted his fruit trees, when Adonis counted his flowers. It was here that a smooth surface afforded my practising Muse a space greatly strengthened by a vast roller. The surface is confined and adorned in a long border and equidistantly on both sides by plants inhabited by a variety of flowers. But who could relate the marvels of the hedge so well groomed? With its dense foliage evenly cut it reveals on its very summit a herd of green wild beasts made from shrubs, the playful work of a hand talented and amazingly skillful in its beautiful pretense that the shapes of Naso have returned.

Do you hear how leafy Hylax barks upon the threshold? Look! He is preventing the animals from entering and is threatening the boys. Here you may see the Nemean lion roaring once again; here on the other side recurs the club of Hercules: moreover opposite, the Hydra hisses but not from a single throat, rising up in her rage, a monster that can be restored. Here you may see stags tossing their antlers on high, and does cropping the acres of a field made out of a tree. Look! A leafy hunter stands by, his reins held loose, poised in expectation and gazing intently as a Gallic hound threatens a hare from behind.

But why should I attempt to express each individual scene in verse? Whatever Maeonides engraved upon the armor of Achilles or the Ascraean bard engraved upon the shield of Hercules—all that could be seen there inwoven in the trimmed shrubbery. The invigorating sequence of scenes cites the authors as authority.

Nemesis at One's Back

In the territory of Elto at the top of a lofty mountain where a path leads toward the citadels of those who dwell amid the rocks, there is a rock of three feet implanted in the ground, not unwelcome to the horseman when he wants to descend a mountain slope on foot and with his neck still intact. Perhaps Mercury positioned this or Terminus in days of old; or by chance it was in this spot that Astraea abandoned the Earth, marking her final footsteps by a rock of no great size.

Once upon a time (so they say) a villain, an evil inhabitant of this countryside, stole a sheep from the neighboring sheepfold. He tied the four-footed beast together and raised it up upon his neck and shoulders. He was going along happily having acquired his booty and availing of the darkness (thus far did the beautiful Laverna smile upon his prayers), but he did not escape, nor did he get away with his theft without being punished. For once when he had climbed a slope, panting and exhausted, he sat down here upon the ground and lying back against the rock, he propped the sheep up against it. As soon as the sheep had found rest, longing to

libertate frui cupiens, conamine toto
movit se, aversa saxique in parte pependit,
raptoremque sui pedibus complexa ligatis
adstrinxit saxo, lictoris munere fungens. 20
nec sivere illum iugulo depellere nodum
exhaustae vires et anhelitus interclusus.
deprensus sedet ergo miser, dum vita per auras
concedit moesta ad manes corpusque reliquit.

Imminet a tergo Nemesis; scelus est sibi lictor. 25
saepe solet Numen crudos punire nocentes,
ac poenas mediis iuvat inseruisse triumphis.

enjoy freedom, it stirred itself with every effort and lay hanging on the opposite side of the rock. Entangling its own abductor in its tied feet, it bound him to the rock, performing a Lictor's duty. His exhausted strength would not allow him to release the noose from around his throat and he became breathless and stifled. And so the wretch sits there entrapped until his miserable life departed through the breezes to the spirits of the dead, and abandoned his body.

Nemesis looms behind. Each man's crime is his own Lictor. It is the frequent custom of the Divinity to punish the savagely guilty, and she delights in sowing punishment in the midst of triumphs.

APPENDIX 2

SULEY BOWLING GREENE

(Bodl. MS Eng. Misc. d.1, ff 45-47)

Suley Bowling Greene

Bod MS Eng. Misc. d.1, ff 45-47

Nigh to the bankes of Avon, where the streame
By neighbour hills compell'd does beare the yoake,
And Wanford owes its credit to the bridge;
Close by a wood upon a mountaines top
There is a place, which tow'ards the South and East   5
With a delightfull prospect doth command
The subject Vales, and pleasant villages,
With territories of farr distant fields.
This plat of old paid tribute to the plow,
But ever since it was inclosed with   10
A quicksett hedge, and clad in velvet green,
It is for sport and triumph sett apart,
And wondring does new husbandmen behold
Cloath'd, not in leather, but in flameing gold.
This first they shave, then with a mighty rolle   15
(Not now [as earst] of wood, but massy stone)
They leavell, smooth, and polish, till they leave
Not the least rub to check the sliding bowle.
   Hither the Gentry, when they would with play,
Unbend theire cares, on a sun-shiny-day,   20
Twice in a week resort; and presently
Divide themselves for York and Lancaster;
But blesse them from the Furies, which those names
Did once imploy! and from base Avarice too;
This many times doth raise ungentle heats   25
Yet neither do I them require to play.
For nothing else but reputation;
"A little quickens art, but too much game
Turnes play to labour, pleasure into paine."
But I that ancient custom much commend,   30
Which setts a double prize, by which they both
The Victors crown, and comfort them that lose.
   But, Boy, come, bring the bowles rub'd shining bright,
Which lead (infusd into one side) hath taught
A steady motion, and a winding path.   35
There joines unto the greene a little house
A pleasant shade against the parching sunne.
This is the place, wherein the boy doth keep
By night, as in a field, his wooden sheep.
   Then first of all the Noble Sylvius   40
Enters the lists, renowned for his skill
I' th' bowling art; well knew he how to lay
A modest touche by the Mistresse side;

Appendix 2

As well he knew with a sure-leveld blow
Out of the field to chase his rival foe. 45
Haveing first plac'd the Trigg he presently
Cast forth a little bowle, which was to bee
The mark, the Mistresse, which they were to winn;
Her all devoutly court, and happy hee
Who can at last the nearest to her bee. 50
Then taking bowle in hand he with his ey
Designs the path wherein his bowle should goe,
And bowing towards the Mistresse gently sends
A message by his bowle, which swims along
The grassy plaine, and by the Mistresse lies. 55
 Him Nisus undertakes second to none
For faire delivery, and a winning cast;
Knocking away a bowle, or throwing farr.
He weigheth forth a lesser-biast bowle,
Which with a narrower and stiffer throw 60
Beares off the former bowle, and takes his place.
 This raised various motions in the breasts
Of the concerned, Anger, griefe, hope, feare,
Shame, indignation, and desire of praise.
Some to mainteine what they had lately gott, 65
And others to recover what they lost;
None wanted courage to defend their side
But none could equallize theire Leaders skill.
 One to increase the triumph, eager was
At least to lay a second; throwes, and then 70
With hue and cry pursues his fleeing bowle;
Now rub he cryes, and reynes it with his voyce;
Then the poor block reviles as dull and slow,
Exhorts, advises, praises it, and with
His writhed body shewes it how to shunn 75
The way-laid rocks, and doth himself persuade
He hath reform'd it by his good advice.
What is't men cannot in a dreame believe?
 Another fully thinking to have thrown
Nisus down head-long from the taken wall, 80
Looses his bowle and strength; Yet bravely done
"However! Nothing venture, nothing have!"
 But as the Roman youth, when once they see
Theire General endangerd in the camp,
Unto his Tent from Every part they run 85
To guard him with theire bodies and theire lives:
Just so is Nisus guarded round about
By his companions, blocking up the wayes
And passages, where danger might approach.
 I would be in vaine to tell of all the rest, 90
Who all miscarried, though in sundry waies!
One's overthrown, and leaves the marke behind;
Another throws halfway; whether it were

Because he threw but faintly, or because
The bowle at setting out tooke double goale.   95
This man throws heavnly wide; and that cutts narrow;
A third man getts his bias wrong, and then
They all laugh at him till they splitt again.
    When Sylvius perceivd that there was none
Left of his party, who could succour bring   100
To his forlorn affaires, and lost estate,
He neither lost his courage, nor curs't Fate,
But gladly the occasion did embrace,
As a fitt scene to shew his vertu on.
"Valour by difficulty is improoved,   105
As streames swell higher, when by Dams opposed."
Then viewing well the place if he could spy
And probe a passage with his searching ey;
"Come on," said he, "Valour can make its way."
    So said he, and then calling for his bowle,   110
Which he on purpose had reservd till now;
With all his might he threw it, and it flew
As if it had bin from some engine sent,
Breaking the hostile troops, and flinging death,
Like some granade, round where e're it went;   115
And having made its way through all delayes
It tooke the Mistresse thence, and handing her
To th'end o'th' greene, there rested at her feet.
    Forthwith the company gave such a shout
As made the heavens ring; and round about   120
The mountaine low'd; so did the frighted herds,
The rarified aire let fall the birds
Thinking they had bin shott; the tattling Dame
Rouz'd out o'th' neighbouring woods, amazed came,
Nor that she e're had heard, could she recall,   125
So greate a triumph when a Stagg did fall.

APPENDIX 3

DILLINGHAM'S OCCASIONAL LATIN VERSE

Dillingham's Occasional Latin Verse

The vigor and inspiration of the Muse of Dillingham's twilight years become all the more evident when the original Latin poems discussed in the present study are compared to his earliest extant Latin verse: three highly conventional pieces that appeared in print between the years 1654 and 1660 and which would not be anthologized in the *Poemata Varii Argumenti*. All three are occasional poems included in Cambridge collections of either funerary or celebratory verse: 1) a funeral elegy on the death of Thomas Gataker (1654), 2) a lament on the death of Oliver Cromwell (1658), 3) a poem in celebration of the Restoration (1660).

(a) On the Death of Thomas Gataker

In Funere Thomae Gatakeri S.T.B.
Viri Doctissimi
Octogenarii Vegeti et Venerandi Senis

Qualiter ales Arabs longae pertaesa senectae
   et cupiens vitam morte parare novam,
undique congesto pretiosa in funera thure,
   ardet in optato victima grata rogo:
sic inter sacros famae et virtutis odores   5
   exuvias ponis tu, Gatakere, tuas.
spiritus eluso tumulo remeavit ad astra;
   circumfert nomen Fama per ora virum.
tu magnus quoties evolvitur Antoninus,
   scilicet a doctis usque legere viris.   10
non tua sat tristi deflerem funera versu
   sufficeret totas si mihi Camus aquas.
ast aliqua volui cineres tibi spargere gutta;
   hanc tibi non ficti pignus amoris habe.[1]

[On the Death of Thomas Gataker S.T.B.,
A Most Learned Individual, An Energetic Octogenarian
and Venerable Old Man

Just as the Arabian bird, thoroughly wearied with a lengthy old age and longing to obtain new life through death, heaps up incense from all sides for its expensive funeral and burns as a welcome victim upon the pyre for which it has yearned, so, Gataker, do you place your spoils amid the hallowed fragrances of fame and virtue. Your spirit has escaped the tomb and has returned to the stars. Fame circulates your name upon the lips of men. Indeed you will continue to be read by learned men as often as Antoninus the Great is unfolded. I could not bewail your death in verse that is sufficiently sad even if the Cam were to supply me with all its waters. But I wanted to besprinkle your ashes with a drop of some sort; have this as the pledge of a genuine affection.]

---

[1] Text is that of Simeon Ashe, *Gray Hayres Crowned with Grace: A Sermon Preached ... at the Funerall of ... Mr Thomas Gataker* (London, 1655), 65-66.

Appendix 3

Dillingham's first published Latin poem is a funeral elegy on the death of Thomas Gataker (1574-1654). A learned scholar, clergyman and preacher, Gataker had strong Cambridge connections (BA 1594; MA 1597; BD 1604; Fellow of Sidney Sussex College from 1596). Among his prolific output are twenty-four tracts and sermons published between 1619 and 1627, a series of funeral orations, collected sermons (published 1637),[2] Latin treatises on the tetragram (1645)[3] and on diphthongs (1646),[4] sermons against antinomianism (1645)[5] and most notably his full-scale edition of Marcus Aurelius, the product of forty years' research.[6] His death occurred on 27 July 1654, just a few weeks before his eightieth birthday. Dillingham's poem appears as the first of eleven such tributes (seven in Latin; four in English composed for the most part by Cambridge academics and acquaintances), which were appended to Simeon Ashe's *Gray Hayres Crowned with Grace: A Sermon Preached ... at the Funerall of ... Mr Thomas Gataker* (1655).[7] As such they take their place within a seventeenth-century Cambridge context and indeed seem to mirror sentiments expressed not only in Ashe's funerary oration, but also in Gataker's own published sermons.

Entitled *In Funere Thomae Gatakeri S.T.B. Viri Doctissimi Octogenarii Vegeti et Venerandi Senis*, Dillingham's piece turns to the world of Latin elegy (reflected in his atypical recourse to elegiacs) to depict its subject as a second phoenix now weary of old age and longing to acquire new life in death, piling up incense for its funeral and then burning upon its pyre. For Gataker such incense constitutes the sacred fragrances of fame and virtue, which he accumulated in life, a life that, like the phoenix, is now reborn on a celestial plain as his spirit has eluded the tomb and has made its way to the stars above. Yet his fame will live on, so the speaker states, through his writings, especially his edition of Marcus Aurelius, and his volumes, which will be read by scholars. The poem concludes in a conventional expression of grief: no verses could adequately convey this mourner's sorrow (even if the river Cam were to supply him with all its waters). Nonetheless this lament is presented as a pledge of genuine affection.

The very title of the poem, with its emphasis on the vigorous and reverend nature of an old man (*vegeti et venerandi senis*) and by implication of old age in general, may reflect Gataker's own comments on the subject. For example his sermon *Abrahams Decease* (on the death of Richard Stock) had proclaimed: "Old age is honorable. Yea, as the Apostle saith of Marriage, 'It is honourable among all men.' It is a 'resemblance' of 'Gods antiquitie,' who is called 'the Ancient of daies.' The glory

---

[2] *Certain Sermons, First Preached and After Published at Severall Times by M. Thomas Gataker* (London, 1637).

[3] *De Nomine Tetragrammato Dissertatio* (London, 1645).

[4] *De Dipthongis* (London, 1646).

[5] *Antinomianism Discovered and Confuted* (London, 1645).

[6] *Marci Antonini Imperatoris de Rebus Suis* (Cambridge, 1652).

[7] Ashe, *Gray Hayres Crowned with Grace*, 65-80.

of young men is their strength: (saith Solomon) and the beauty of old men is the gray-head. And, old age or the gray-head is a crowne of glory, that is a glorious crowne, where it is found in the way of righteousness."[8] The theme lies at the very heart of Ashe's funeral speech, which takes as its biblical point of departure *Proverbs* 16.31: "The hoary head is a Crown of glory, if it be found in the way of righteousness,"[9] proclaiming: "The beauty of old men is the gray-head. And the Apostle Paul speaketh of his old age as his credit, and that which should render him the more respectfull."[10] It is a speech that appropriates the whole to Gataker himself: "his hoary-head was a Crown of glory, for it was found in the way of righteousnesse. Through God's good providence, he had a long time worn this his Crown, for he was well nigh Fourscore years old."[11] Likewise James Duport's verse tribute appended to Ashe's sermon describes Gataker as a *reverendus ... senex* possessing *vigor* and a *vegetam viridemque senectam*.[12]

The poem's opening lines are characterized by their oxymoronic tone: the desire to prepare for new life through death (*cupiens vitam morte parare novam* [2]), the presentation of a willing victim of death who finds a funeral pyre for which he longs (*optato victima grata rogo* [4]). Such a tone likewise underlines Gataker's "Pious Epigram," which prefaces the collected laments. Thus: "I thirst for thirstiness; I weep for tears" (1); "I cannot choos but live, because I die" (5).[13] More specifically, Gataker had conveyed something of that paradoxical quest for life through death in such homiletic writings as *Abraham's Deceased*: "For this life here, is in a manner no life; it is life in name, but in deed and truth, death. It is no true life that cannot overcome death, that yeeldeth to, that tendeth to, that endeth in death,"[14] and *The Decease of Lazarus*: "They dye not, though they dye: death is no death to them: as they hope even in death; so they live even in death. As others are dead while they live; so they live when they dye. As to the worldly their life is but a passage unto death; so to the godly their death is but an entrance into life: their deaths-day is better to them

---

[8] *Abrahams Decease: A Meditation on Genesis 25.8 Delivered at the Funerall of that Worthy Servant of Christ Mr Richard Stock* (London, 1627), 48.

[9] Ashe, *Gray Hayres Crowned with Grace*, 1.

[10] Ashe, *Gray Hayres Crowned with Grace*, 11.

[11] Ashe, *Gray Hayres Crowned with Grace*, 38.

[12] James Duport, *In Obitum Reverendi Admodum Senis*, 70-71: *atque vigorem aequans vegetaque viridique senecta/ingenio florens etiam vergentibus annis* (Ashe, *Gray Hayres Crowned with Grace*, 68). Cf. a certain A.M's lament entitled *Desiderium* 24: *raramque simul in senectute senectutem* (Ashe, *Gray Hayres Crowned with Grace*, 69).

[13] "A Pious Epigram of Mr Gataker" (Ashe, *Gray Hayres Crowned with Grace*, 65).

[14] Gataker, *Abrahams Decease*, 44-45.

than their birth-day: it is the birth-day of their immortality, the birth-day of their eternity."[15]

Central to the oxymoron of Dillingham's poem is the figure of the phoenix now wearied of old age (*longae pertaesa senectae* [1]) and in search of another life. Simeon Ashe repeatedly conveys Gataker's own rather impatient eagerness to leave this mortal life and find rest in heaven. Thus: "'I expect daily, yea hourly to be translated into that everlasting rest, which God hath prepared for them who are interested in his Christ.' These were his last words unto me ..."[16] Then just prior to his death: "July 26: Early in the morning, full of pain, gasping and panting, he cried out 'How long Lord, how long? Come speedily,'"[17] and finally "July 27: Within an hour after, nature being quite spent, he gave up the Ghost, and was translated into that Rest which he so often and earnestly had desired to finde in another world, because he could obtain none in this."[18]

While the equation of Gataker with the phoenix likewise occurs in Thomas Ducard's lament ("A perfect Body of Divinity,/And such a Phoenix" [44-45]),[19] its role as a Christian symbol of resurrection and afterlife finds an interesting neo-Latin parallel in John Milton's *Epitaphium Damonis*, a lament on the poet's close friend Charles Diodati. Here an ekphrasis depicting the phoenix looking back at a rising dawn serves to convey the envisaged resurrection of Diodati in a Christian heaven.[20] But Gataker has also achieved a form of earthly immortality, guaranteed through his scholarly writings. Just as the phoenix accumulates incense for its *pretiosa ... funera* (3), so has Gataker laid his *exuvuiae* (6) among his learned works. This is his earthly treasure so to speak. Or in the words of Simeon Ashe: "He was not so great a Treasurer, as a free dispenser of those riches of the minde, which he did communicate readily, expeditely, cleerly."[21] Chief among these is *Magnus ... Antoninus* (9), a work

---

[15] Gataker, *The Decease of Lazarus Christs Friend. A Funerall Sermon on John Chap. 11. vers. 11 Preached on the Buriall of Mr John Parker* (London, 1640), 23.

[16] Ashe, *Gray Hayres Crowned with Grace*, 39.

[17] Ashe, *Gray Hayres Crowned with Grace*, 60.

[18] Ashe, *Gray Hayres Crowned with Grace*, 61.

[19] Thomas Ducard, "On the Death of the most Reverend, Learned, Holy Mr Thomas Gataker," 44-45 (Ashe, *Gray Hayres Crowned with Grace*, 72).

[20] Cf. Milton, *Ep. Dam.* 185-189: *in medio Rubri Maris unda, et odoriferum ver,/littora longa Arabum, et sudantes balsama silvae/has inter Phoenix, divina avis, unica terris,/caeruleum fulgens diversicoloribus alis,/Auroram vitreis surgentem respicit undis*. Text is that of *John Milton: Minor Poems*, ed. John Carey (Longman, 1997).

[21] Ashe, *Gray Hayres Crowned with Grace*, 62. On the implementation of the metaphor of treasure, cf. James Duport, *Gray Hayres Crowned with Grace*, 67, lines 41-42: *sic ille, Hesperiae ditatus munere gazae;/nec minus ex Oriente potens*; Thomas Ducard, "On the Death of the Most Reverend ... Gataker," 5-6: "And were not Death well undergone to save/So great a Treasure from the hungry Grave?"; 81-82: "As the

likewise singled out by several of the other contributors. Thus James Duport states: *nunc etiam cordi est Aurelius unus et alter/quos ille inter se solerti indagine mentis/comparat, et quantum deficerit Antoninus/advertit,*[22] while a certain A.M. extols the edition as follows: *nobilem tandem et ultimum en tibi laborem,/(certo oculis nostris ultimum)/Antoninum Optimum Maxumum,/(ingens imperii decus, et Musarum delicias.*[23] For, as Simeon Ashe had stated, "Although he be now dead, yet he still liveth by his worthy Works already printed."[24]

(b) On the Death of Cromwell

> Quicquid apud veteres miramur turba nepotum,
>   Graecorum quicquid Romulidumve Ducum,
> Caesar, Alexander, Pompeius, quotquot ab armis
>   argumenta suae nobilitatis habent,
> Scipio, Marcellus, Fabii, queis mascula virtus   5
>   pro patriae lata nomina fecit ope,
> et si quod reliquum est nomen virtutis: in uno
>   conduntur tumulo, Magne Olivere, tuo.
> te dominum, teque orba suum dolet Anglia natum,
>   te Protectorem Musa Fidesque suum.   10
> gentis honos, belli fulmen legumque satelles,
>   virtutis custos et stupor orbis eras.
> Magne, vale, Cromwelle, vale; nunc ergo coronam
>   quo minus accipias nil prohibere potest.
>   *Pax et Salus erat Oliverus Angliae,*   15
>   *Hoc nos fatemur, hoc loquentur posteri;*
>   *Adeste cives, efferamus patriam.*
> at tu, qui tanti succedis Principis haeres,
>   quem poscit dominum terra Britanna suum,
> macte animo et virtute tua, sis mactus honore,   20
>   deliciae gentis praesidiumque tuae.
> tu, Ricarde, reges patriis virtutibus orbem,
>   dum populo praestas otia, iura, fidem.
> quin faveas foveasque tuas, Ricarde, Camoenas;
>   sic erit et posthac quae tua gesta canat.[25]   25

---

most golden Key that ere was made/To open Gods deep Treasure therein layd" (Ashe, *Gray Hayres Crowned with Grace*, 71 and 73).

[22] James Duport, *In Obitum Reverendi Admodum Senis*, 50-53 (Ashe, *Gray Hayres Crowned with Grace*, 67-68).

[23] A.M., *Desiderium* 45-48 (Ashe, *Gray Hayres Crowned with Grace*, 70).

[24] Ashe, *Gray Hayres Crowned with Grace*, 40.

[25] Text is that of *Musarum Cantabrigiensium Luctus et Gratulatio* (Cambridge, 1658), *4^v-A1^r.

[Whatever aspect of the ancients, whatever aspect of the leaders of the Greeks or of Romulus's sons inspires the wonder of us, the throng of their descendants; however many the proofs of their own nobility in warfare possessed by Caesar, Alexander, Pompey, Scipio, Marcellus, the Fabii, whose manly bravery made their fame widespread for the assistance they brought to their country, and whatever fame for bravery that might remain: all these are buried in that single tomb of yours, Oliver the Great. A bereaved England laments you, her Lord, you, her own son; the Muse and the Faith lament you, their own Protector. You were the glory of your nation, a thunderbolt of war, the upholder of laws, the custodian of virtue and marvel of the world. Farewell, Cromwell the Great, farewell; for now there is nothing that can prevent you from receiving a crown.

> Oliver was England's Peace and Salvation. This let us confess, of this let posterity speak. Be at hand, citizens, let us extol our country.

But you who succeed as heir to a Prince so great, you whom the land of Britain calls for as its Lord, honorable in mind and in your virtue, may you be honorable in glory, the beloved and the protection of your nation. May you, Richard, rule the world with your father's virtues while you provide your people with peace, justice, faith. Furthermore may you look with favor upon and cherish your own Muses. In this way there will survive one to sing your exploits hereafter.]

Three years later there appeared in the *Musarum Cantabrigiensium Luctus et Gratulatio* (Cambridge, 1658), Dillingham's Latin elegy on the death of Oliver Cromwell. The piece assumes a rather conventional place in a multilingual university collection of predominantly Latin, but also Greek,[26] Hebrew,[27] and English[28] epicedia on the deceased Protector. Indeed the bipartite nature of Dillingham's poem (lines 1-17 on the death of Oliver; 18-25 on his successor Richard) would seem to mirror aspects of the volume itself—a volume whose title-page with its contrasting nouns *luctus* and *gratulatio* reflects a twofold purpose: 1) to lament the death of Cromwell

---

[26] Greek poems are provided by R. Widdrington (*Musarum Cantabrigiensium Luctus et Gratulatio*, A2^v), J. Cremer (*Musarum Cantabrigiensium Luctus et Gratulatio*, D2^r), R. Critton (*Musarum Cantabrigiensium Luctus et Gratulatio*, D4^r), and Charles Darby (*Musarum Cantabrigiensium Luctus et Gratulatio*, F1^v-F2^r). Two of the poems (by R. Widdrington [*Musarum Cantabrigiensium Luctus et Gratulatio*, A3^r] and R. Bowen [*Musarum Cantabrigiensium Luctus et Gratulatio*, F3^v]) combine both Latin and Greek.

[27] See R. Cudworth (*Musarum Cantabrigiensium Luctus et Gratulatio*, *3^v).

[28] See Thomas Fuller (*Musarum Cantabrigiensium Luctus et Gratulatio*, G3^r-G3^v), G.G. (*Musarum Cantabrigiensium Luctus et Gratulatio*, G3^v-G4^r), Charles Darby (*Musarum Cantabrigiensium Luctus et Gratulatio*, G4^v-H1^r), R.H.C.J. (*Musarum Cantabrigiensium Luctus et Gratulatio*, H1^r), B. Turner (*Musarum Cantabrigiensium Luctus et Gratulatio*, H1^v-H2^r), Dawson (*Musarum Cantabrigiensium Luctus et Gratulatio*, H2^r-H2^v), and Samuel Fuller (*Musarum Cantabrigiensium Luctus et Gratulatio*, H2^v-H4^v).

(*Illa in Funere Oliveri*)[29] and 2) to acclaim his successor (*Haec De Ricardi Sucessione Felicissima Ad Eundem*).

In many respects the piece sits quite happily alongside others in a somewhat conventional collection,[30] which typically convey in rhetorical hyperbole the grief felt by England upon the death of this heroic or quasi-heroic figure. Thus, like the majority of epicedia it reverts to traditional elegiacs,[31] and compares the deceased to figures from a classical, and more specifically Roman, world. This Romanization of the whole is perhaps best conveyed in the words of an anonymous contributor, who states that in comparison to Oliver's achievements all the marvels of the Roman race should fall silent.[32] Dillingham states that whatever constituted Roman virtue[33] is buried in Oliver's tomb.[34]

One of the leitmotifs of the volume is the depiction of Oliver as a second Caesar. Thus Charles Darby asks: "For where is Rome if Caesar be not there."[35] The theme is perhaps most fully developed by Samuel Fuller: "When Caesar dy'd then

---

[29] The title page misprints *Ille* for *Illa*.

[30] Some less conventional elements in the collection include the pastoral setting of the whole provided by Anon. at F3^v-F4^r, as Tityrus is urged to proclaim the death of Daphnis amid a pastoral landscape characterized by pathetic fallacy. Striking too is a certain Dawson's depiction of Oliver waging wars on a cosmic and quasi-celestial level (H2^r-H2^v).

[31] Contrast, however, the neo-Horatian poems by R. Huckle (*Musarum Cantabrigiensium Luctus et Gratulatio*, B2^r-B3^r); Anon. (*Musarum Cantabrigiensium Luctus et Gratulatio*, B3^v-B4^r); Bernard Skelton (*Musarum Cantabrigiensium Luctus et Gratulatio*, C1^r-C1^v); Robert Quarles (*Musarum Cantabrigiensium Luctus et Gratulatio*, F1^r); J. Cutlove (*Musarum Cantabrigiensium Luctus et Gratulatio*, F4^v-G2^r).

[32] *Omnia Romanae sileant miracula gentis,/queis animis par est Herculeusque labor* (C3^v).

[33] On a syntactical level the rhetorical opening of Dillingham's poem with its inverted syntax and *quicquid* (1; 2) *quotquot* (3) and *si quod* (7) clauses, which are resolved only in line 8, is paralleled by John Pratt's Latin piece, which opens with a series of *quas ... qui ... quod* clauses (A2^r).

[34] On the tomb motif, cf. Charles Darby: "See, how whole Brittain strives to be his Urn;/And, while his dolefull Funerals do burn,/Is strew'd with ashes, like the neighb'ring plains,/'Mongst which the fiery mouth'd Vesuvius reigns./At Westminster, me thinks, I see each Tomb,/And statue brustle, for to make him room;/Wiping their dustie faces, that they might/Behold so rare a Monarch; at whose sight/All bow themselves, and that subjection own,/Which, had they liv'd with him,/they must have done" (G4^v-H1^r). Cf. B. Turner "Nature's distrest, thy Grave seemeth to be/Th' last gasp her honour hath, inter'd in thee" (H1^v).

[35] *Musarum Cantabrigiensium Luctus et Gratulatio*, G4^v.

Tybers tide did rise"[36] now replaced by "the Caesar of our time."[37] As Caesar he passes on his dominion to his "son," a second Augustus.[38] Other contributors compare him to such mythological Roman heroes and deities as Atlas,[39] Hercules,[40] and Mars.[41] But quite striking in Dillingham's poem is the rather condensed *Romanitas* and pseudohistoricism of the whole as Cromwell is compared to such classical "heroes" as Alexander, Pompey, Scipio, Marcellus, and the Fabii. In none of the other poems is there such *variatio* in terms of classical personae. But like the other contributors Dillingham echoes commonplace sentiments, lauding "Mighty Oliver" (*magne Olivere* [8])[42] as a thunderbolt of war (*belli fulmen* [11]),[43] the custodian of laws (*legumque satelles* [11]),[44] and the envisaged recipient of a heavenly crown (13-14).[45] Several contributors depict Richard Cromwell as a phoenix rising from his

---

[36] *Musarum Cantabrigiensium Luctus et Gratulatio*, H2^v.

[37] *Musarum Cantabrigiensium Luctus et Gratulatio*, H3^r. Cf. "This world is bigge with Cesars, and indeed/Contains more Heroes than the Trojan steed" (*Musarum Cantabrigiensium Luctus et Gratulatio*, H3^v).

[38] Thus Thomas Arrowsmith: *felix/Iulius Augusto commisit regna* (E1^r); Thomas Resbury: *non aliter Magnus concessit Iulius, amplum/imperii molitus opus; cum Roma subactos,/Augusto regnante, per otia despicit hostes* (E4^v).

[39] Cf. Thomas Resbury: *par Atlas humeris* (E4^r); R. Powell: *magnum prius Atlas/ tantum sensit onus* (F2^r).

[40] For R. Powell he surpasses Hercules: *credo fuisse, fides si danda laboribus, ipsum hunc/de caelo reducem, maioremve Hercule* (F2^r).

[41] Cf. B. Turner: "Mar's own Generalissimo here is,/Wars Genius, Arthur's Metempsychosis./With fire and sword Hannibal hewing down/The Alps of opposition to a Crown" (H1^v).

[42] Cf. Thomas Resbury: *laetus, Magne, tuas accedo ad Aras* (E4^r); Thomas Fuller describes hope as: "Great as thy self, Great Oliver" (G3^r); Samuel Fuller: "Here lies Great Oliver" (H3^v)

[43] Cf. Richard Minshull: *quem Mars haud valuit funestis sternere telis* (*1^v); G. Moses: *vindice Cromuello, Mars ferus ipse fugit* (A1^r); G. Horne: *vis pugnae, belli gloria, Martis amor* (D1^v); J. Layton: *consiliis nova regna pater firmavit honestis,/et Martis simul et Palladis arma tulit* (E1^v); G.G.: "Mars envy'd thee, nor can we blame him for't;/He found a rival in Bellona's court;/Saturn in brazen walls thou didst confine,/Joves thunder was not so much feard as thine" (G4^r).

[44] Cf. G. Leigh: *Legum veneranda fides* (B1^r).

[45] Cf. T. Rolle: *maluit in caelo placidam traducere vitam/et semper viridi cingere fronde comam* (C2^v); G.G.:"Since all things do remain serene and calm,/Hang Cypress by; conquests are crown'd with palm./Cease whining griefs, and let's rejoyce, that he/Is Deifi'd in Heavens Hierarchy" (G4^r); R.H.C.J.: "Mount O Seraphick soul,

father's ashes.[46] For others he is equated with the sun-god Phoebus.[47] Dillingham's emphasis on the importance of Richard's moral virtue (*macte animo et virtute tua sis, mactus honore* [20]) is paralleled by E. Bachiler: *macte animi, princeps, sequere et vestigia patris:/sic Numa eris vita, moribus atque Cato.*[48] His description of Richard as *deliciae gentis praesidiumque tuae* (22) finds a parallel in G. Leigh: *deliciae populi, Patriae spes una, salutis/depositum nostrae, Pacis sanctissime Custos.*[49] In the poem's closing lines the son is exhorted in neo-Virgilian terms to rule the world with his father's virtues: *reges patriis virtutibus orbem* (22)[50] and to favor and foster the Muses.[51] Thus will Richard's exploits be sung.[52]

---

advance a Throne/Above the shade of earths dark gloomy Cone:/Highness it self to Climb is no low thing,/For Heaven is preferment for a King./Ascend then Noble soul the highest Sphere,/They reach a note far above Ela there./March on th' Etherial fields, the Angels will/With silver trumpets sound an Onset, till/You scale those walls" (I1^r).

[46] Cf. Anthony Tuckney: *ecce! Novus Cromuellus adest e funere patris/Phoenix de Phoenice novi reparabilis aevo* (*1^r); G. Horne: *alterius Phoenix oritur per funera: nec dum/secula Phoenices ulla tulere duos* (D1^v); G. Perse: *Phoenixque paterno/nascitur e busto* (D4^v); Turner Jr: *extincti Phoenix patris redivivus ab urna* (E2^r); Charles Darby: *mortuus est Phoenix: at dum iacet inter odores,/exsurgit soboles digna parente suo./occidit illustris Phoebus: caligo minatur/pluribus; et tenebras Anglia tota timet:/At novus exoriens radiis fulgentibus orbem/lustravit* (F1^v); T. Haymes: *occidit una licet, surgit tamen altera Phoenix,/alternaque nitet Phoebus uterque vice* (F4^v); J. Cutlove: *busto emicans Phoenix parentis* (G2^r).

[47] Cf. Thomas Arrowsmith: *rursus gestit ovans Phoebum agnovisse recentem* (E1^r); J. Layton: *nove Phoebe* (E1^v); Thomas Fuller: "Methinks I see a Rising Sun display/His golden beams, and chase those clouds away./It is illustrious Richard, justly fit/For th'Princely seat, whose soul can equal it" (G3^v).

[48] *Musarum Cantabrigiensium Luctus et Gratulatio*, C4^v.

[49] *Musarum Cantabrigiensium Luctus et Gratulatio*, B1^v; Cf. SSJC: *deliciae populi, vita, salusque sui* (D3^v).

[50] Cf. W. Preston: *viva [sic], decus magnum praesidiumque tuis/I bone, quo virtus tua te vocat, I pede fausto* (C2^v); G. Horne: *alter Cromuellus patriis virtutibus haeres/accedit, cuius spirat in ore pater* (D1^v); J. Layton: *tu quoque, successor menti regnoque paterno,/sceptra tibi grata tradita pace regas* (E2^r); Thomas Fuller: "Since He, and all his virtues lie in Thee" (G3^v).

[51] Cf. Anthony Tuckney: *sacris praestabit et otia Musis* (*1^r); G. Horne: *te posse Ducem, Musisque vacare/scimus, qui afflictis ante patronus eras* (D1^v).

[52] Cf. R. Widdrington: *more Patris Grantam si protegis, illa Camoenis,/cum moreris, faciet ne moriare suis* (A3^r).

Appendix 3

(c) **On The Restoration**

Ad Serenissimum Carolum II,
Angliae, Scotae, Franciae et Hiberniae Regem,
Fidei Defensorem &c.

Accipies humiles (Rex Augustissime) Musas,
    quas tibi Grantigenae porrigit unda Cami.
accipe, sed vultu quo nos aspexeris olim
    quum placuit nostram nobilitare togam;
qua tu fronte beas Anglos coelumque serenas,   5
    et populo laetos promis ab axe dies.
en proreptantes tristi de nocte sorores
    ut possint Phoebo te propiore frui!
tu placido aspectu faveas (nil amplius optant),
    illae etenim vultu stantque caduntque tuo.   10
ecce triumphalem nectit tibi Musa coronam,
    imponitque tuis officiosa comis.
erepta accipitri dulcis philomela triumphat
    gratum soteri et fundit ab ore melos.
Harpyiarum ungues cum nos iam iamque tenerent,   15
    Caesar ades vindex; hinc tibi Σωστρα damus.
Carole, tu redimis Musas ornasque redemptas,
    sic pulchre munus protegis ipse tuum.
"Carole vive diu," coelorum cura, tuique
    Deliciae populi, "Carole vive diu."[53]   20

[To the Most Serene Charles II,
King of England, Scotland, France and Ireland,
Defender of the Faith &c.

May you receive, your Majesty, the lowly Muses which the waters of Cam's river Grant offer you. Receive them but with that countenance with which in times past you looked upon us when it was your pleasure to ennoble our gown; with that expression with which you bless the English, make calm the sky, and bring forth from the heavens days of joy for your people. Look at the sisters creeping their way out of the grim of night in order to be able to enjoy the closer presence of you, their Phoebus! May you look favorably upon them with gentle aspect (nothing more do they desire) for it is by your countenance that they both stand and fall. Behold, the Muse is weaving a triumphal crown for you and is dutifully placing it upon your locks. The nightingale sings her sweet triumph at her escape from the hawk as from her lips she pours forth a melody pleasing to her savior. When the claws of the Harpies were now all but holding us, you are at hand, an avenging Caesar; hence we bestow *Sostra* upon you. Charles, it is you who rescue the Muses and having rescued them, you adorn them. In this splendid manner do you protect your own gift. "Long live Charles," an object of care to the heavens, and your people's beloved, "long live Charles."]

---

[53] Text is that of *Musarum Cantabrigiensium Sostra*, (Cambridge, 1660), *3[r].

It was in 1660 that Dillingham composed a Latin verse encomium addressed to Charles II. This short poem introduces the *Musarum Cantabrigiensium Sostra* (Cambridge, 1660), a multilingual volume (Latin, Greek, Hebrew) of university verse celebrating the Restoration. Read alongside such contributions, Dillingham's piece is characterized by a typical air of graceful formality appropriate to a poem intended no doubt to encapsulate the spirit of the volume as a whole. Indeed where such contributors as William Fairebrother and James Duport had founded their pieces upon such witty anagrammatic punning as Charles Stuart/*stet lar charus* or *Carolus Stuart*/*At Tu Ros Clarus*,[54] Dillingham seems content to assume a rather conventional and dutiful place in a seventeenth-century royalist world.

The poem's opening lines present the collection as an offering to the king from the river Cam at Granta: *Musas/quas tibi Grantigenae porrigit unda Cami* (1-2)[55] for this is a patron who has ennobled Cambridge University, here described metonymically as "our ... toga"—a reference to the academic gown: *quum placuit nostram nobilitare togam* (4).[56] This is reflected in several of the other contributions that depict him as, for example, the *desiderium populi, gentisque togatae*[57] or as a second Apollo acknowledged as such by the university as a whole: *teque suum agnoscit Grantana Academia Phoebum*.[58] The choice of deity has a twofold purpose. On the one hand, it equates the king with the god of poetry; on the other it evokes the light-bring, life-giving force of a sun-god, dispersing the darkness and creating a new dawn. The latter theme, which functions as a virtual leitmotif of the volume, seems to underlie Dillingham's statement that Charles blesses the English people and calms the sky, and that he brings forth propitious days: *qua tu fronte beas Anglos coelumque serenas,/et populo laetos promis ab axe dies* (5-6). The whole is developed later as the Parcae are envisaged as creeping their way out of the darkness of the underworld in order to enjoy the radiance of Charles, their new Apollo (*en proreptantes tristi de nocte sorores/ut possint Phoebo te propiore frui!* [7-8]).[59] The equation of the king

---

[54] See *Musarum Cantabrigiensium Sostra*, (Cambridge, 1660) D3^v and O4^v respectively.

[55] On references to Cam and Granta, cf. Theoph. Dillingham: *vestes coccineas iam soror utraque/gestet, Granta suas, Oxonium suas* (*Musarum Cantabrigiensium Sostra*, B1^r); R. Chrichton: *ut spes Granta Parens concipit Alma novas!/qui modo pene metu belli glaciante rigebat,/atque piger fragili constitit amne latex/Musarum de fonte salit, ducitque choreas/incipit et liquidis ludere Chamus aquis* (*Musarum Cantabrigiensium Sostra*, L1^v).

[56] Cf. M. Thruston: *gentisque imprimis Academica turba Togatae,/ordo omnis sexusque omnis* (*Musarum Cantabrigiensium Sostra*, E1^v).

[57] T. Gearing, *Musarum Cantabrigiensium Sostra*, K2^v.

[58] James Duport, *Musarum Cantabrigiensium Sostra*, O4^v.

[59] Worthy of comparison perhaps is the contribution by Francis Hughes, which draws a striking contrast between Charles's monarchy and the dominion of the Parcae, praying that the royal scepter may reign over their very spindles: *ecce premit solium*

with Apollo or the sun likewise occurs in poems by a certain Antonius (of Trinity College),[60] Theoph. Dillingham,[61] J. Worthington,[62] N. Wragge,[63] Thomas Horton,[64] Richard Kitson,[65] Robert Alfounder,[66] and Owen Hughes[67] inter alios.[68] But this is a king who has a very close relationship with the Muses. Dillingham asks that he show favor to the Muses since it is by his countenance that they either stand or fall: *tu placido aspectu faveas (nil amplius optant),/illae etenim vultu stantque caduntque tuo*

Carolus, premat usque precamur,/Parcarum et fusos regia sceptra regant (*Musarum Cantabrigiensium Sostra*, C3^v).

[60] Cf. *ut lux post longas oritur mage grata tenebras/sic tu, Car'le, tuis gratissimus advena terris/... cum tu Sol oreris, sunt omnia protinus alba/Sol oriens* (*Musarum Cantabrigiensium Sostra*, *3^v).

[61] *qualiter apparens post tristia nubila Phoebus/splendidius laeto fundit ab ore iubar* (*Musarum Cantabrigiensium Sostra*, B1^r).

[62] *tu simul ac nostro praesentior orbe refulges,/diffugiunt tenebrae, Carole, luce nova,/ecce horas, nulla temeratas nube, serenas!/en placidos soles, candidiusque iubar!* (*Musarum Cantabrigiensium Sostra*, B1^v). Cf. Anon.: *redde diem: radios petit alma Academia vestros,/nam nova lux oculis est inimica suis* (*Musarum Cantabrigiensium Sostra*, C2^r).

[63] *tuis affulgeat Anglis/clarior e tenebris, fato sublimior omni/maiestas* (*Musarum Cantabrigiensium Sostra*, C3^v).

[64] *aspicis ut nigram radiis clarissima noctem/subsequitur tenebras sole fugante dies* (*Musarum Cantabrigiensium Sostra*, A2^v).

[65] *vidimus lucem tenebris fugari;/vidimus solem rediisse, claro/cuius adventu fugiunt ab altis/montibus umbrae* (*Musarum Cantabrigiensium Sostra*, D1^v).

[66] *sed tandem nostris illucet Phosphorus oris,/Auroram ostendens extremo a margine coeli,/et portas soli paulatim pandit, at ille/purpureus pede primo attingens limen Olympi/omnia perfundit laeto splendore* (*Musarum Cantabrigiensium Sostra*, I4^r).

[67] *salve festa dies, rosea quae lampade primum,/sidereo, et nostri Caesaris ore nites* (*Musarum Cantabrigiensium Sostra*, K3^r).

[68] Cf. M. Thruston: *salve, o formosum iubar! O laetabile lumen!/exoreris tandem, ac manifesto numine fulgens/discutis horrendas tenebras* (*Musarum Cantabrigiensium Sostra*, E1^v); Fr. Bridge: *parce tuis (Princeps) radiis, Phoeboque minori/assuetas placidus da posse accedere Musas* (*Musarum Cantabrigiensium Sostra*, I4^v); R. Boys: *Musa negat: sed Apollo iubet, mihi magnus Apollo/Carolus exoriens, omnia luce beans* (*Musarum Cantabrigiensium Sostra*, L1^r); R. Chrichton: *qualis purpuream sparsurus ab aequore lucem/Phoebus anhelantes aureus urget equos,/talia purpurea tu maiestate decorus/rex auguste, diem reddis ab oceano* (*Musarum Cantabrigiensium Sostra*, L2^r); John Boult: *et ille melior dum refulget Cynthius* (*Musarum Cantabrigiensium Sostra*, M4^r).

(9-10).⁶⁹ Likewise Robert Grove hails him as *o sacra Maiestas, tu Musis divus Apollo,/tu stator populis Iupiter esto tuis*.⁷⁰ In Dillingham, this special relationship between king and Muses (symbolic here of seventeenth-century poets in particular and perhaps of the poetic art in general) will constitute a key element of the poem's climactic triumph: *Carole, tu redimis Musas ornasque redemptas,/sic pulchre munus protegis ipse tuum* (17-18). But even before this Charles's anticipated acts of favor and patronage are reciprocated by the Muse herself, who is already weaving him a crown of triumph and placing it upon his hair: *ecce triumphalem nectit tibi Musa coronam,/imponitque tuis officiosa comis* (11-12). This poetic coronation mirrors the very act of the Cambridge *Sostra* and its verse encomia of the restored king, but it also recalls such classical celebrations of military triumphs as those enjoyed by Caesar.⁷¹ For this is a national hero who has rescued England now envisaged as a nightingale snatched from the claws of an eagle and pouring forth a song of thanksgiving to her savior: *erepta accipitri dulcis philomela triumphat/gratum soteri et fundit ab ore melos* (13-14). Then in a fusion of the historical and mythological Charles is described as an heroically vindictive Caesar⁷² delivering the nation from the claws of the Harpies (*Harpyiarum ungues cum nos iam iamque tenerent,/Caesar ades vindex* [15-16]). While the Harpy theme likewise occurs in two contributions by M. Barlow,⁷³ and William Leigh respectively,⁷⁴ the equation with Augustus Caesar is to be found in poems by Richard Kitson,⁷⁵ Thomas Gale,⁷⁶ Robert Grove,⁷⁷ R.

---

⁶⁹ Cf. Radulphus Widdrington: *Carolus est, semperque fuit, cui serviet uni/Doctrinae Musis quicquid et artis inest* (*Musarum Cantabrigiensium Sostra*, A4ʳ).

⁷⁰ *Musarum Cantabrigiensium Sostra*, E3ʳ.

⁷¹ Cf. Richard Love: *da modo, da facilis tua cingant tempora, princeps,/tum vel Caesareas vincent fulgore coronas* (*Musarum Cantabrigiensium Sostra*, A1ʳ).

⁷² This classicizing of the whole is evident in other contributions that equate Charles with such heroic figures as Hercules (*Anglicus Alcides* [by a certain J.B., *Musarum Cantabrigiensium Sostra*, N3ʳ]) or Aeneas (*et velut Aeneas terris iactatus et undis/moenia conspexit tandem promissa Lavini,/optatas Britonum Carolus sic conspicit oras:/quo Phoebo in nostro coelo splendente vocemur/nunc iterum minima contenti nocte Britanni* [R. Nevile, *Musarum Cantabrigiensium Sostra*, M1ᵛ]).

⁷³ *Harpyiasque truces delusit hiantes,/faucibus eripuitque bolum, certumque triumphum* (*Musarum Cantabrigiensium Sostra*, B4ᵛ).

⁷⁴ William Leigh: *quae non mala sensimus Angli? ... Harpyarumque rapaces/ungues* (*Musarum Cantabrigiensium Sostra*, G1ᵛ).

⁷⁵ *sic tuos inter vigeas Britannos,/Caesar et terris dominare felix;/divus ut sero redeas in altos,/Carole, coelos* (*Musarum Cantabrigiensium Sostra*, D2ʳ).

⁷⁶ *Caesarem vehis; modo/sistas, quo placuit, litore debitum/terris, debita caelo/iuxta Phasiacam* (*Musarum Cantabrigiensium Sostra*, D4ᵛ).

⁷⁷ Thus England is stablized by *Caesaris adventu* (*Musarum Cantabrigiensium Sostra*, E3ʳ).

Chrichton,[78] inter alios. It is an equation that is hardly surprising, given the fact that Augustus had delivered the Roman nation from the horrors of civil war. Charles is thus punningly hailed as *rex augustissime*,[79] endowed with the Augustan appellation *pater patriae*,[80] and even envisaged by several contributors as surpassing his classical counterpart.[81] Dillingham's poem concludes with the conventional "Long Live the King": *"Carole vive diu," coelorum cura, tuique/deliciae populi, "Carole vive diu"* (19-20),[82] repeated twice in hymnic salutation.[83]

---

[78] *Caesare venturo, visuri ad littora passim/hinc atque hinc vulgi confluit unda frequens ... Caesar ter maxime* (*Musarum Cantabrigiensium Sostra*, L2^r).

[79] E. Foxcroft.: *rex augustissime* (*Musarum Cantabrigiensium Sostra*, K3^r).

[80] Rudulphus Widdrington: *ille Pater Patriae, legum veneranda potestas ... ut levis Augustam ventilet aura ratem* (*Musarum Cantabrigiensium Sostra*, A4^v).

[81] Thus Andrew Yardley: *Carolus Augusto sit uti felicior, et tu,/qui dictus olim es optimus* (*Musarum Cantabrigiensium Sostra*, I3^v); John Boult: *Augustiorem ... Caesarem* (*Musarum Cantabrigiensium Sostra*, M3^v).

[82] Cf. B. Whichcot: *Carole vive diu* (*Musarum Cantabrigiensium Sostra*, A3^r); H. Masterson: *vive Deo gratus Carole, vive pius* (*Musarum Cantabrigiensium Sostra*, B2^r); M. Thruston: *vive diu Magni proles genuina Parentis* (*Musarum Cantabrigiensium Sostra*, E2^r); T. Gearing: *hactenus Anglorum suspiria, verba precesque,/nunc demum excipias, Carole vive diu* (*Musarum Cantabrigiensium Sostra*, K2^v).

[83] On hymnic repetition, cf. Richard Love: *Carolus ecce redit, regni tutela salusque ... Carolus ecce redit, pietatis cultor avitae* (*Musarum Cantabrigiensium Sostra*, A1^r), and, on a elaborate level the refrain *rerum praeside Carolo* in Theoph. Dillingham's piece (*Musarum Cantabrigiensium Sostra*, B1^r).

BIBLIOGRAPHY

1. MANUSCRIPTS

British Library, London.

BL Harley 7052
BL Sloane 1710.
BL Sloane 1766.
BL Sloane 1815.

Bodleian Library, Oxford.

Bodl. MS Eng. Misc. d.1.
Bodl. MS Tanner 39.
Bodl. MS Tanner 48.
Bodl. MS Tanner 40.
Bodl. MS Tanner 44.
Bodl. MS Tanner 63.
Bodl. MS Tanner 147.

2. PRIMARY TEXTS

ALBERTI, Leon Battista, *Hypnerotomachia Poliphili* (Venice, 1499).
ASHE, Simeon, *Gray Hayres Crowned with Grace: A Sermon Preached ... at the Funerall of ... Mr Thomas Gataker* (London, 1655).
BACON, Francis, *The Essayes or Counsels, Civill and Morall*, ed. Michael Kiernan (Oxford, 1985).
BATHURST, Theodore, *Calendarium Pastorale sive Aeglogae Duodecim, Totidem Anni Mensibus Accommodatae. Anglice olim Scriptae ab Edmundo Spensero Anglorum Poetarum Principe: Nunc autem Eleganti Latino carmine donatae a Theodoro Bathurst* (London, 1653).
BEDFORD, Arthur, *Lusus Pilae Palmariae* in *Selecta Poemata Anglorum, Seu Sparsim Edita, Seu Hactenus Inedita*, ed. Edward Popham (Bath, 1774-1776), I, 43-47.
BENTLEY, Samuel, *Poems on Various Occasions: Consisting of Original Pieces and Translations* (London, 1774).
BOURNE, Vincent, *Poematia, Latine Partim Reddita, Partim Scripta: a V. Bourne, Collegii Trinitatis Apud Cantabrigienses Aliquando Socio* (London, 1734).
——————, *Poematia, Latine Partim Reddita, Partim Scripta: a V. Bourne, Collegii Trinitatis Apud Cantabrigienses Aliquando Socio Tertio Edita Adiectis ad Calcem Quibusdam Novis* (London, 1743).
CAMDEN, William, *Britannia: Or a Chorographical Description of Great-Britain and Ireland* (London, 1735).

COTTON, Charles, *The Compleat Gamester: Or Full and Easy Instruction for Playing at Above Twenty Several Games Upon the Cards* (London, 1726).
COWPER, William, *Poetical Works*, ed. H.S. Milford (Oxford, 1971).
CULVERWELL, Nathaniel, *Spiritual Opticks: or a Glasse Discovering the Weaknesse and Imperfection of a Christians Knowledge in this Life* (Cambridge, 1651)
————, *An Elegant and Learned Discourse of The Light of Nature* (London, 1652)
DALLAWAY, James, *Anecdotes of the Arts in England* (London, 1800).
DALLINGTON, Robert, *Hypnerotomachia: The Strife of Love in a Dreame* (London, 1592).
DEZALLIER D'ARGENVILLE, Antoine-Joseph, *The Theory and Practice of Gardening* (London, 1728).
DILLINGHAM, William, *Aegyptus Triumphata* (London, 1680).
————, *A Sermon at the Funeral of the Lady Elisabeth Alston* (London, 1678).
————, *Poemata Varii Argumenti Partim e Georgio Herberto Latine (Utcunque) Reddita, Partim Conscripta a Wilh. Dillingham, S.T.D.* (London, 1678).
DUPORT, James, *Ecclesiastes Solomonis* (Cambridge, 1662).
DYER, John, *Poems 1761* (Scolar Press: London, 1971).
ELIOT, T.S., *Four Quartets* (London, 1979).
ERASMUS, *De Civilitate Morum Puerilium Per D. Erasmum Roterodamum Libellus* (London, 1578).
EVELYN, John, *Diary*, ed. E.S. De Beer (Oxford, 1955).
————, *Silva or a Discourse of Forest-Trees* (York, 1786).
Fables for Youth (London, 1777).
FERRARIUS, Philip, *Lexicon Geographicum* (London, 1657).
FLACCUS, Valerius, *Argonauticon*, ed. Peter Langen (Hildesheim, 1964).
FOUCAULT, Michel, *Language, Counter-Memory, Practice: Selected Essays and Interviews*, trans. D.F. Bouchard and Sherry Simon (Ithaca, 1977).
GATAKER, Thomas, *Abrahams Decease: A Meditation on Genesis 25.8 Delivered at the Funerall of that Worthy Servant of Christ Mr Richard Stock* (London, 1627).
————, *Antinomianism Discovered and Confuted* (London, 1645).
————, *Certain Sermons, First Preached and After Published at Severall Times* (London, 1637).
————, *De Dipthongis* (London, 1646).
————, *De Nomine Tetragrammato Dissertatio* (London, 1645).
————, *Marci Antonini Imperatoris de Rebus Suis* (Cambridge, 1652).
————, *The Decease of Lazarus Christs Friend. A Funerall Sermon on John Chap. 11. vers. 11 Preached on the Buriall of Mr John Parker* (London, 1640).
HALL, John, *Poems* (Cambridge, 1646).
HARRISON, Janet, "The Tall One Isn't Moving," *College English* 32.8 (1971), 951.
HAWES, Stephen, *The Pastime of Pleasure*, ed. W.E. Mead (London: Early English Text Society, 1928).
HENTZNER, Paul, *A Journey into England in the Year MDXCVIII* (Twickenham, 1757).
HESIOD, *The Homeric Hymns and Homerica*, trans. H.G. Evelyn-White (Cambridge, Mass., 1977).
HOOD, Thomas, *The Complete Poetical Works*, ed. Walter Jerrold (London, 1906).
HOMER, *Iliad*, trans. A.T. Murray, rev. W.F. Wyatt (Harvard: Loeb Classical Library, 1999).
HOMER, *Odyssey*, trans. E.V. Rieu (Penguin, 1966).
HORACE, *Epodes*, ed. David Mankin (Cambridge, 1995).

HORTON, Thomas, *Choice and Practical Expositions on Four Select Psalms* (London, 1675).
―――, *Forty-six Sermons upon the Whole Eighth Chapter of the Epistle of the Apostle Paul to the Romans* (London, 1674).
HOWLETT, Robert, *The School of Recreation, or, A Guide to the Most Ingenious Exercises of Hunting, Riding, Racing, Fireworks, Military Discipline, The Science of Defence, Hawking, Tennis, Bowling, Ringing, Singing, Cock-Fighting, Fowling* (London, 1698).
ISHAM, Thomas, *The Diary of Thomas Isham of Lamport (1658-81), Kept by Him in Latin from 1671-1673 at His Father's Command*, trans. Norman Marlow, with notes and commentary by Sir Giles Isham (Farnborough, 1971).
LANDOR, Walter Savage, *Poemata et Inscriptiones* (London, 1847).
LELAND, John, *The Itinerary ... In Or About the Years 1535-1543*, ed. Lucy Toulmin Smith (London, 1907).
LOVECHILD, Mrs., *A Miscellany in Prose and Verse for Young Persons* (London, 1795).
LUCRETIUS, *De Rerum Natura Libri Sex*, ed. Cyril Bailey (Oxford, 1963).
LYTTON, E.R. Bulwer, "The Chess Board" in R.M. Leonard, ed., *A Book of Light Verse* (Oxford and London, 1910), 147.
MAHONY, F.S., "The Shandon Bells" in R.M. Leonard, ed., *A Book of Light Verse* (Oxford and London, 1910), 355.
MAJOR, William, *Four Satires Translated from the Latin into English Verse. To which are Added Some Occasional Poems on Various Subjects by a Gentleman, Late of Balliol College, Oxford* (London, 1743).
MARCHANT, John, *Lusus Iuveniles or Youth's Recreation* (London, 1753).
MARSHALL, William, *Planting and Ornamental Gardening: A Practical Treatise* (London, 1785).
MASON, William, *The English Garden* (London, 1777-81).
MILTON, John, *Minor Poems*, ed. John Carey (Longman, 1997).
NORFOLK, Charles Howard, *Historical Anecdotes of Some of the Howard Family* (London, 1769).
ORWELL, George, *Nineteen Eighty-Four*, ed. Bernard Crick (Oxford, 1984).
OVID, *Amores, Medicamina, Faciei Femineae, Ars Amatoria, Remedia Amoris*, ed. E.J. Kenney (Oxford, 1994).
―――, *Metamorphoses*, ed. W.S. Anderson (Teubner, 1977).
―――, *Tristia, Ibis, Ex Ponto, Halieutica, Fragmenta*, ed. S.G. Owen (Oxford, 1963).
PLINY the Elder, *Historia Naturalis*, ed. and trans. A.E. Pépin (Paris, 1947).
PLINY, the Younger, *Epistularum Libri Decem*, ed. R.A.B. Mynors (Oxford, 1963).
POPE, Alexander, *Rape of the Lock*, ed. Cythia Wall (Boston and New York, 1998).
―――, *The Prose Works*, ed. Norman Ault (Oxford, 1936).
RAY, John, *Historia Plantarum Generalis, Species Hactenus Editas Aliasque Insuper Multas Noviter Inventas et Descriptas Complectens* (London, 1693-1704).
RUDDER, Samuel, *A New History of Gloucestershire. Comprising the Topography, Antiquities, Curiosities* (Cirencester, 1779).
SENECA, *Ad Lucilium Epistulae Morales*, ed. L.D. Reynolds (Oxford, 1965).
SERVIUS, *In Vergilii Bucolica et Georgica Commentarii*, ed. George Thilo (Teubner, 1887).
SEYMOUR, Richard, *The Compleat Gamester* (London, 1739).
SHELLEY, Percy Bysse, *The Poetical Works*, ed. Mary Wollstonecraft Shelley (London and New York, 1889).

SOMERVILE, William, "The Bowling Green," *Occasional Poems, Translations, Fables, Tales &c.* (London, 1727), 67-80.
STEWART, Dugald, *Elements of the Philosophy of the Human Mind* (London, 1792-1827).
SUETONIUS, *Divus Augustus (De Vita Caesarum Liber II)*, ed. M.A. Levi (Florence, 1951).
The Elegant Entertainer, and Merry Story-teller: Being a Valuable Collection of Diverting and Instructive Tales, Fables, and Other Curious Articles, Both in Prose and Verse (London, 1676).
The Spectator, ed. D.F. Bond (Oxford, 1965).
Vere, Francis, *The Commentaries* (Cambridge, 1657).
VIDA, Marco Girolamo, *Scacchia Ludus*, ed. with introduction and notes by M.A. Di Cesare (*Bibliotheca Humanistica & Reformatorica* 13: Nieuwkoop, 1975).
VIRGIL, *Aeneid*, ed. R.D. Williams (New York, 1982), 2 vols.
——————, *Eclogues*, ed. Robert Coleman (Cambridge, 1977).
——————, *Georgics*, ed. R.F. Thomas (Cambridge, 1988), 2 vols.
WHITE, Thomas, *Tintinnalogia or The Art of Ringing* (London, 1671).
WORDSWORTH, William, *Poems*, ed. J.O. Hayden (Penguin, 1977).

3   ANTHOLOGIES

'Ανθολογία *seu Selecta Quaedam Poemata Italorum qui Latine Scripserunt* (London, 1684).
Carmina Illustrium Poetarum Italorum, ed. G.G. Bottari (Florence, 1689-1775).
Delitiae Carminum Italorum Poetarum Huius Superiorisque Aevi (Frankfurt, 1608).
Delitiae Carminum Poetarum Belgicorum Huius Superiorisque Aevi (Frankfurt, 1612).
Delitiae Carminum Poetarum Gallorum Huius Superiorisque Aevi (Frankfurt, 1609).
Delitiae Carminum Poetarum Germanorum Huius Superiorisque Aevi (Frankfurt, 1612).
Eighteenth-Century Poetry, eds. David Fairer and Christine Gerrard (Oxford: Blackwell, 2004).
Examen Poeticum Duplex (London, 1698).
Musarum Anglicanarum Analecta (Oxford, 1699).
Musarum Anglicanarum Analecta (London, 1741).
Musarum Cantabrigiensium Luctus et Gratulatio (Cambridge, 1658).
Musarum Cantabrigiensium Sostra (Cambridge, 1660).
Selecta Poemata Italorum qui Latine Scripserunt, cura cuiusdam Anonymi Anno 1684 Congesta, Iterum in Lucem Data, Una Cum Aliorum Italorum Operibus, Accurante A. Pope (London, 1740), 2 vols.
The Oxford Book of Eighteenth Century Verse, ed. D.N. Smith (Oxford, 1936).

4 SECONDARY LITERATURE

AURIGEMMA, Salvatore, *The Baths of Diocletian and the Museo Nazionale Romano*, trans. J. Guthrie (Fifth edition Rome: Istituto Poligrafico Dello Stato, 1963).

BAKER, Margaret, *Discovering Topiary: The History and Cultivation of Clipped Hedges and Trees* (Hertshire, 1969).

BATTISTI, Eugenio, "Natura Artificiosa to Natura Artificialis." *The Italian Garden*, ed. David Coffin (Washington: Dumbarton Oaks Colloquium, 1972), 3-36.

BERETTA, Ilva, "The World's a Garden": *Garden Poetry of the English Renaissance* (Uppsala, 1993).

BRADNER, Leicester, *Musae Anglicanae: A History of Anglo-Latin Poetry 1500-1925* (London and New York, 1940).

BRAYBROOKE, "Hangman Stones," *Notes and Queries* 1 (May 31, 1856), 435.

CASTELL, Robert, *The Villas of the Ancients* (London, 1728).

CLARK, Elizabeth, "George Herbert and Cambridge Scholars," *George Herbert Journal* 27 (2006), 43-52.

DE FOREST LORD, George, *Heroic Mockery: Variations on Epic Themes From Homer to Joyce* (New Jersey: Associated University Presses, 1977).

DICK, B.F., "Vergil's Pastoral Poetic: A Reading of the First *Eclogue*," *American Journal of Philology* 91 (1970), 277-293.

FARRAR, Linda, *Ancient Roman Gardens* (Sutton Publishing, 1998).

GATTY, Alfred, "Hangman Stones," *Notes and Queries* 1 (June 21, 1856), 502-503.

GENTZLER, Edwin, *Contemporary Translation Theories* (London and New York, 1993).

GREAVES, C.S.,"Churchdown: Similar Legends at Different Places," *Notes and Queries*, 1 (January 5, 1856), 15-16.

HAAN, Estelle, *Classical Romantic: Identity in the Latin Poetry of Vincent Bourne* (Transactions of the American Philosophical Society 97.1 [Philadelphia, 2007]).

——————, "Ringing Classical Bells?: Virgilian Intertexts in Dillingham's *Campanae Undellenses*," *Notes and Queries* 54.4 (December, 2007), 425-428.

——————, *Thomas Gray's Latin Poetry: Some Classical, Neo-Latin and Vernacular Contexts* (Brussels: Collection Latomus 257, 2000).

——————, *Vergilius Redivivus: Studies in Joseph Addison's Latin Poetry* (Transactions of the American Philosophical Society 95.2 [Philadelphia, 2005]).

HAINSWORTH, Peter and ROBEY, David, eds., *The Oxford Companion to Italian Literature* (Oxford, 2002).

HALE, J.K., *Milton's Languages: The Impact of Multilingualism on Style* (Cambridge, 1997).

HARGREAVES, Cecil, *A Translator's Freedom: Modern English Bibles and Their Language* (Sheffield, 1993).

H.E.C., *Notes and Queries* 1 (May 31, 1856), 435-436.

HEINEKEN, N.S., "The Hangman-stone," *Notes and Queries* 1 (May 17, 1856), 402.

HUNT, John Dixon, "Evelyn's Idea of the Garden: A Theory for All Seasons," in *John Evelyn's Elysium Britannicum and European Gardening*, eds. Therese O'Malley and Joachim Wolschke (Washington, 1998), 269-288.

KELLIHER, W.H. *Oxford Dictionary of National Biography*, eds H.C.G. Matthew and Brian Harrison (Oxford: Oxford University Press, 2004), sv William Dillingham.

KELLY, L.G., *The True Interpreter: A History of Translation Theory and Practice in the West* (Oxford, 1979).

LAWSON, James, "The Roman Garden," *Greece and Rome* 19.57 (1950), 97-105.

LAWSON, William, *A New Orchard or Garden* (London, 1618), ed. Eleanour Sinclair Rohde (London, 1927).
LAZZARO, Claudia, *The Italian Renaissance Garden* (New Haven and London, 1990).
LEFAIVRE, Liane, *Leon Battista Alberti's Hypnerotomachia Poliphili: Re-Cognizing the Architectural Body in the Early Italian Renaissance* (Cambridge, Mass., 1995).
MARTINDALE, Charles, "Green Politics: The *Eclogues*," in *The Cambridge Companion to Virgil*, ed. Charles Martindale (Cambridge, 1997), 107-124.
———, ed. *The Cambridge Companion to Virgil* (Cambridge, 1997).
MONEY, David, *The English Horace: Anthony Alsop and the Tradition of British Latin Verse* (Oxford: Oxford University Press, 1998).
MYERS, K. Sara, "*Docta Otia*: Garden Ownership and Configurations of Leisure in Statius and Pliny the Younger," *Arethusa* 38 (2005), 103-129.
MCALEER, E.C., "Understanding 'The Shandon Bells,'" *Modern Language Notes* 66.1 (1951), 474-475.
NEVILE, Jennifer, "Dance and the Garden: Moving and Static Choreography in Renaissance Europe," *Renaissance Quarterly* 52.3 (Autumn 1999), 805-836.
NIDA, E.A., *Toward a Science of Translating: With Special Reference to Principles and Procedures Involved in Bible Translating* (Leiden, 1964).
NIELSEN, Inge, *Thermae et Balnea* (Denmark, 1993).
PAGÁN, V.E., *Rome and the Literature of Gardens* (Duckworth, 2006).
PARKER, Deborah, *Lectura Dantis: Inferno X*, in *Lectura Dantis* 1. no. 1 (Fall, 1987), 37-47.
PERKELL, Christine, "On *Eclogue* 1. 79-83," *Transactions of the American Philological Association* 120 (1990), 171-181.
PEROSA, Alessandro, *Giovanni Rucellai ed il suo Zibaldone* (London, 1960).
PHILLIPS, J.W., "Similar Legends at Different Places," *Notes and Queries* 14, (April 5, 1856), 282.
ROSS, Stephanie, *What Gardens Mean* (Chicago, 1998).
SCHULTE, Rainer and BIGUENET, John, eds., *Theories of Translation: An Anthology of Essays from Dryden to Derrida* (Chicago, 1992).
SEGAL, C.P., "*Tamen cantabitis, Arcades*: Exile and Arcadia in *Eclogues* 1 and 9," *Arion* 4 (1965), 237-266.
SEMLER, L.E., "Robert Dallington's *Hypnerotomachia* and the Protestant Antiquity of Elizabethan England," *Studies in Philology* 103.2 (2006), 208-241.
SHUCKBURGH, E.S., *Emmanuel College* (London, 1904).
STRONG, Roy, *The Renaissance Garden in England* (London, 1979).
WARD, John, *Roman Era in Britain* (Methuen: London, 1911).
WATERS, R.E.C., *Genealogical Memoirs of the Extinct Family of Chester of Chicheley* (London, 1878).
WIDMAYER, A.F., "Mapping the Landscape in Addison's 'Pleasures of the Imagination,'" *Rocky Mountain Review of Language and Literature* 50.1 (1996), 19-29.

INDEX NOMINUM

Abraham, 99, 100
Achilles, 32, 71, 74
Actium, 73
Adam, 67
Addison, Joseph, 9, 17, 18, 20, 21, 22, 23, 25, 26, 27, 28, 30, 31, 33, 34, 35, 36, 68-69
Adonis, 70
Aeneas, 29, 32, 33, 43, 52, 73, 74, 110
Aeolus, 46
Africans, 42
Ajax, 31
Alberti, Leon Battista, 64
Alciato, Andreas, 60
Alcinous, 69, 70
Alexander the Great, 102, 103, 105
Alfounder, Robert, 109
Alps, 105
Alsop, Anthony, 8
Alston, Elisabeth, 5
Alston, Thomas, 6
Amazon, 35
Anchises, 31
Anna, 43
Antilochus, 29
Antoninus, 98, 99, 101-102
Apollo, 20, 30, 56, 57, 72, 106, 107, 108, 109, 110
Arabia, 98, 101
Aratus, 74
Arcadia, 42
Arrowsmith, Thomas, 105, 106
Arthur, 105
Ashe, Simeon, 98-102
Astraea, 56
Atlas, 105
Atterbury, Francis, 8
Aurelius, Marcus, sv Antoninus
Ausonia, 23
Avon, river, 22, 23, 25, 45

Bachiler, E., 106
Bacon, Francis, 66
Barberini, Maphaeus, 65
Barclay, William, 7
Barlow, M., 110
Barnsley, 59
Barnwell, 3, 43
Bartassius, 14, 15
Basto, 35

Bathurst, Theodore, 4, 10, 24
Battus, 57
Bedford, Arthur, 18, 26, 29, 33, 35
Belgium, 1
Belinda, 35
Bellona, 105
Bentley, Samuel, 19, 20, 21, 22, 23, 24, 25, 26, 27, 28, 30, 31, 32, 36
Beza, Theodore, 2, 7
Blenheim, 68
Boult, John, 109, 111
Bourne, Vincent, 9, 13, 14, 39, 40, 45, 47
Bowen, R., 103
Boys, R., 109
Bridge, Fr., 109
Brighton, 59
Britons, 42
Buchanan, George, 2

Cacus, 57
Caesar, Augustus, 34, 46, 69, 73, 105, 109, 110, 111
Caesar, Julius, 102, 103, 104, 105, 107
Calcagnini, Caelio, 55, 60
Calliope, 46
Cam, river, 41, 98, 99, 107, 108
Cambridge, 1, 2, 3, 4, 5, 6, 9, 10, 12, 41, 46, 54, 98-111
Camden, William, 65
Canterbury, 3
Capilupus, Laelius, 8
Casa, Giovanni, 44
Castor, 52
Cato, 106
Cerberus, 72
Chaderton, Laurence, 6
Charles II, King, 45, 46, 107-111
Chester, 5
Chicheley, 5
Chrichton, R., 108, 109, 111
Christ, Jesus, 5, 101
Cicero, 63
Cirencester, 58
Cloanthus, 33-34
Colonna, Francesco, 64
Colyton, 58
Conti, Natale, 7, 8
Corydon, 37
Cotton, Charles, 22, 30, 31

Cowper, William, 47
Cremer, J., 103
Cremona, 2
Critton, R., 103
Cromwell, Oliver, 98, 102-106
Cromwell, Richard, 102, 103, 105, 106
Cudworth, R., 103
Culverwell, Nathaniel, 4
Curll, 34
Curtius, Marcus, 5
Cutlove, J., 104, 106
Cypress, 72

Dactius, Andreas, 60
Daedalus, 52-55
Dallaway, James, 68
Dallington, Robert, 64
Dante, 27
Daphne, 30, 72
Daphnis, 42, 72, 104
Darby, Charles, 103, 104, 106
Darwin, Erasmus, 73
David, 2
Dawson, Mr, 103, 104
Deiopea, 46
Denham, John, 12
Derbyshire, 58
Dido, 29, 43, 45, 46
Dillingham, Theoph., 108, 109, 111
Dillingham, Thomas (Sr.), 3, 43
Dillingham, Thomas (Jr.), 6
Dillingham, William,
— *Ad Serenissimum Carolum II*, 107-111
— *Aegyptus Triumphata*, 6
— *A Sermon at the Funeral of the Lady Elisabeth Alston*, 5
— *Avicula*, 2, 14, 43, 49-55, 86-87
— *Campanae Undellenses*, 2, 9, 39-47, 49, 80-85
— *In Funere Oliveri Cromuelli*, 102-106
— *In Funere Thomae Gatakeri*, 98-102
— *Nemesis a Tergo*, 2, 15, 49, 55-60, 88-91
— *Sepes Hortensis*, 2, 15, 25, 61-74, 88-89
— *Suleianum*, 2, 9, 14, 17-37, 49, 76-81, 93-96

Diocletian, 35
Diodati, Charles, 101
Ducard, Thomas, 101
Duport, James, 12, 100, 101, 102, 108
Durdens, 17
Dyer, John, 45

Echo, 45
Egypt, 6
Eliot, T.S., 40-41
Elis, 36
Elton, 56
Elysium, 46
England, 2, 4, 8, 10, 17, 20, 21, 23, 46, 57, 64, 65, 68, 102, 103, 104, 106, 107, 110, 111
Entellus, 34
Erasmus, Desiderius, 1, 2
Essex, 59
Euphrates, river, 46
Eurydice, 43-44, 50, 51
Evander, 52
Eve, 67
Evelyn, John, 17, 63, 66

Fabii, 102, 103, 105
Fairebrother, William, 108
Fane, Charles, 22
Ferrarius, Philip, 5
Fisher, John, 62
Flaccus, Valerius, 53
Fletcher, Giles, 7, 8
Fletcher, Phineas, 2, 3
Flora, 25, 64
Florence, 27
Foremark, parish of, 58
Foucault, Michel, 62
Foxcroft, E., 111
France, 1, 107
Friend, Joseph, 18
Frowde, Philip, 18
Fuller, Samuel, 103, 104, 105
Fuller, Thomas, 103, 105, 106

Gale, Thomas, 110
Gataker, Thomas, 98-102
Gearing, T., 108, 111
Genesis, 100
Germany, 1
Ghibellines, 27

Index Nominum

Gibson, Jabez, 59
Gloucestershire, 58
Granta, river, 106, 107, 108
Gray, Thomas, 54
Greece, 60
Grongar Hill, 45
Grotius, Hugo, 2, 3, 9
Grove, Robert, 110
Guelphs, 27
Gyas, 31, 33, 34

Hacket, John, 4
Hall, John, 4, 7
Hampton Court, 65
Hannibal, 105
Harding, Francis, 54
Harpies, 107, 110
Harrison, Janet, 69
Haverfordwest, 58
Hawes, Stephen, 64
Haymes, T., 106
Heinsius, Daniel, 4
Helen (of Troy), 29
Henry VIII, King, 22, 65
Hentzner, Paul, 65
Herbert, George, 1, 9, 10, 11, 12
Hercules, 57, 72, 74, 104, 105, 110
Hermes sv Mercury
Hesiod, 56-57, 74
Hesperia, 101
Hesperides, 70
Homer, 20, 21, 29, 31, 32, 36, 56, 57, 70, 74
Hood, Thomas, 47
Hooke, 9
Horace, 8, 14, 24, 40, 52, 104
Horne, G., 105, 106
Horton, Thomas, 6, 109
Howard, Catherine, 22
Howlett, Robert, 17, 19, 25, 27, 30
Huckle, R., 104
Hughes, Francis, 108
Hughes, Owen, 109
Hydra, 72
Hylax, 71-72

Icarus, 52-55
Ireland, 65, 107
Isham, Justinian, 3, 62
Isham, Thomas, 6, 62

Italy 1, 2, 19, 21, 64, 65, 72
Ithaca, 21, 29, 32

James I, King, 7
Jeremiah, 3
Job, 2
Jonah, 3
Joyce, James, 20
Juno, 46
Jupiter, 20, 36, 105, 110

Keasington, Henry, 59
Kitson, Richard, 109, 110
Knapp, Francis, 18

Landor, Walter Savage, 2
Lane, Francis, 10
Latium, 43
Lawson, William, 66
Layton, J., 105, 106
Lazarus, 100, 101
Lee, river, 44
Leigh, William, 105, 106, 110
Leland, John, 65-66
Lermaeus, Gabriel, 14
Littlebury, parish of, 59
Little Haven, 58
London, 1, 40
Love, Richard, 110, 111
Lovechild, Mrs., 52
Low Countries, 2
Lubcloud, 59
Lucan, 2
Lucina, 24
Lucretius, 72
Lycidas, 42
Lytton, E.R. Bulwer, 20

Mahony, F.S., 43, 44
Major, William, 19
Manilius, 2, 15
Manillo, 35
Marcellus, 102, 103, 105
Marchant, John, 19, 27, 28, 30
Mars, 105
Marshall, William, 66
Mary, Queen, 65
Mason, William, 67
Masters, Thomas, 7, 8, 18, 19, 22, 23, 28, 30, 31, 36

Masterson, H., 111
Mattius, Gaius, 69
Meliboeus, 37, 42, 44
Melvin, Andrew, 2
Menalcas, 42
Menoetes, 31
Mercury, 20, 56, 57
Milton, John, 101
Minshull, Richard, 105
Misenus, 33
Mnestheus, 34
Moeris, 42
More, Thomas, 2
Moses, G., 105

Nautes, 35
Nemean lion, 72
Nemesis, 55-60
Nestor, 29
Nevile, R., 110
Newhaven, 59
Nisus, 32, 33, 34, 35, 36
Nonsuch, 65, 68
Norfolk, Charles Howard, 68
Northamptonshire, 3, 43, 44
Numa, 106
Nymphs, 23, 26, 29, 37, 45, 46, 71

Oaxis, 42
Odell, 6
Odysseus, 56
Olney, 62
Olympus, 42, 109
Orion, 45
Orpheus, 43, 50, 51
Orwell, George, 40
Oundle, 6, 13, 21, 22, 39-47, 62
Ovid, 15, 21, 50, 52-55, 57, 69, 70-74
Oxford, 1, 9, 19, 67-68, 107, 108
Oxley, John of, 59-60

Palaemon, 42
Pallas, 105
Pam, 35
Pareus, David, 7
Parker, John, 101
Patroclus, 32
Paul, Saint, 100
Peleus, 71
Pembroke, 58

Penelope, 21, 29, 32
Perse, G., 106
Perseus, 15
Peterborough, 22
Phoebus, sv Apollo
Pliny, the Elder, 63, 69
Pliny, the Younger, 34, 35, 63, 68, 69, 74
Pluto, 20
Pollux, 52
Pompey, 102, 103, 105
Pope, Alexander, 8, 9, 20, 23, 33, 34, 35, 36, 67, 68
Popham, Edward, 18
Potter, Mr, 59-60
Powell, R., 105
Pratt, John, 104
Preston, parish of, 57-58
Preston, W., 106
Proteus, 30

Quarles, Francis, 19, 30
Quarles, Robert, 104

Ray, John, 63
Resbury, Thomas, 105
Rhaedus, Thomas, 2, 3
Rolle, T., 105
Rome, 2, 12, 13, 14, 15, 18, 36, 44, 45, 51, 60, 62, 69, 104, 105
Romulus, 103
Rotterdam, 1, 2
Rucellai, Giovanni, 65
Rudder, Samuel, 57

Sabrina, 23
Saffron Walden, 59
Salius, 32
Sancroft, William, 3, 5, 6, 8, 9, 11, 12, 13, 44, 49, 51, 52, 53, 54, 55, 56, 61, 73
Saturn, 105
Scipio, 102, 103, 105
Scotland, 2
Scythia, 42
Segnio, Fabio, 70
Seneca, 34
Servius, 69
Seymour, Richard, 19, 27
Shandon, 43, 44

Index Nominum

Sheffield, 59
Shelley, Mary Wollstonecraft, 54
Shelley, Percy Bysse, 54
Sidmouth, 58
Sidney, Philip, 1
Sirens, 65
Skelton, Bernard, 104
Solomon, 12, 100
Somervile, William, 19, 23, 24, 25, 26, 27, 28, 30, 31, 35, 36
Spadillo, 35
Spenser, Edmund, 4, 10, 24
Statius, 68
St Bride's Church, 40, 45
St Clement Danes Church, 40
St Clement's Church, Eastcheap, 40
St Martin-in-the-Fields Church, 40
St Mary-le-Bow Church, 40, 45
St Mary Overie Church, 40
Stewart, Dugald, 31
Stock, Richard, 99, 100
Strada, Firmianus, 15
Suetonius, 34
Sulehay, 17-37, 76-81, 93-96 sv also Dillinhhgham, William, *Suleianum*
Sylvius, 33, 35, 36, 37

Terminus, 56
Thames, river, 40
Theseus, 71
Thetis, 71
Thomson, James, 49-50
Thruston, M., 108, 109, 111
Thuanus, 2, 9
Tiber, river, 105
Tityrus, 23, 44, 104

Toller, Mary, 6
Towy, river, 45
Triton, 33
Troy, 52, 105
Tuckney, Anthony, 106
Turner, B., 103, 104, 105, 106
Tuscany, 63, 74

Ussher, James, 6

Vanbrugh, 68
Vere, Francis, 5
Vida, Marco Girolamo, 2, 3, 14, 19-20, 21
Virgil, 2, 7, 15, 17, 20, 22, 23, 24, 26, 28, 29, 30, 31-34, 36, 37, 41, 42-46, 50-52, 57, 69, 71, 72, 73, 74, 106

Wansford, 22, 25
Watson, Thomas, 20
Westmorland, Earl of, sv Fane, Charles
Whichcot, B., 111
White, Robert, 62
White, Thomas, 39
Widdrington, R., 103, 106, 110, 111
Wild, Robert, 41, 42, 43
William, King, 65
Wilson, Rae, 47
Woodhill, rectory of, 6
Wordsworth, William, 54
Worthington, J., 109
Wragge, N., 109
Wren, Christopher, 40
Wresehill Castle, 65

Yardley, Andrew, 111
Yorkshire, 65

www.ingramcontent.com/pod-product-compliance
Lightning Source LLC
Chambersburg PA
CBHW080801020526
44114CB00035B/4